EVERYBODY'S WOKKING

Martin Yan

Photography by
Geoffrey Nilsen

To you just wokking !

An Astolat Book

HARLOW & RATNER
Emeryville, California

Food Styling:
  Diane Elander

Research and Recipe
Testing: Bernice C. Fong,
  Barbara Goldman, Judith
  Hines, Ivan Lai, Gladys Lee,
  Laura McEwen, Jan Nix,
  Diane Onizuka, Carrie Seeman,
  Susan Yan, Jennifer Yuen

Illustrations:
  Pauline Phung

Design:
  Schuettge & Carleton

Typography:
  Classic Typography

Special Thanks To:
  Jay Harlow, Susan Mattmann,
  Becky Neeley, Rhoda Yee,
  Pam Nagle, Ken Short, Macy's
  California, Takahashi,
  Taylor & Ng, Bernie Schimbke

ISBN 0-9627345-0-0
Library of Congress Catalog Card
Number: 90-84545

Printed in Singapore
10 9 8 7 6 5 4 3

"Soy and Ginger Braised Turkey Breast"
from *The Turkey Cookbook* by Rick
Rodgers. Copyright © 1990 by John
Boswell Management, Inc. Reprinted by
permission of HarperCollins Publishers, Inc.

Harlow & Ratner
5749 Landregan Street
Emeryville, CA 94608

Acknowledgments

With each new cookbook and each new show I come to learn and appreciate the tremendous talents and support contributed by my friends and colleagues. Again they have collectively shaped what was once nothing more than energized confusion into a beautiful book and a series of 26 enjoyable and educational television shows.

Teaching is the greatest means of learning. Through my classes and cooking demonstrations, I have learned a great deal from my own students and from the public. The same can be said about the writing of this book and the production of the new season of the "Yan Can Cook" show. I am indebted to everyone involved in these projects: my tireless recipe testing staff, the talented KQED crew, the creative kitchen staff, and especially Gayle Yamada, whose energy and enthusiasm infused the entire project.

My mother, the only person I know who is faster than me with a cleaver (even with eyes closed), finally made her first visit to the United States during the writing of this book. Over the years, I have drawn much inspiration from her as I have from my wife Sue, and I am forever in debt to both for their patience, support, and vision.

Finally, my thanks go to all of you loyal fans of Yan. I am delighted that the "Yan Can Cook" show has drawn such a wide spectrum of support and enthusiasm. The letters I receive and the responses from our live studio audience are warm and encouraging, and I can never offer enough gratitude for them.

So to all of you, my friends, viewers, colleagues, and family, may you find new joy in your own wok of life. Thanks.

Martin Yan

Contents

Introduction

Over the ten years that "Yan Can Cook" has been on the air, I have watched Asian food and Asian cooking continue to grow in popularity, and with plenty of good reasons. Some people are looking for a more healthful diet, and the traditional Chinese diet is just what the doctor ordered: heavy on the vegetables and grains, with modest amounts of fat, and with meats used in small amounts, mainly as a flavoring ingredient.

Others are drawn to the foods of China, Japan, and other Asian countries for the diversity of flavors. Most major cities have restaurants offering not just generic "Chinese" cuisine, but local and regional specialties of Canton, Shanghai, Sichuan, Hunan, Shandong, and Beijing. Even Cantonese food, the most familiar style to North Americans, is being revitalized by a new generation of immigrants and chefs from Hong Kong and southern China. In many cities, we can eat in restaurants and shop in stores featuring, in addition to Chinese and Japanese foods, the foods of many other Asian countries, including Korea, Thailand, Vietnam, the Philippines, Indonesia, Malaysia, Cambodia—the selection gets bigger every day.

The recipes in *Everybody's Wokking* are designed to offer the reader a wide variety of delicious and healthful Asian dishes that are easy to prepare at home. Some of them are favorites from my family, others have come from my travels throughout Asia. Each year, in addition to visiting my mother in China, I take time to visit various other Asian countries, shopping in the local markets, tasting local food specialties, and working with restaurant chefs. I always end up adding a few dishes to my personal repertoire, bringing them home to share with you, my readers and viewers. In this eighth season of "Yan Can Cook," I have included not only Chinese dishes, but a sampling of new favorites ranging from Korean *bulgogi* (grilled beef with sesame) to Filipino *lumpia* (a delicious variation on spring rolls) to the zesty hot and sour shrimp soup of Thailand.

Of course, I never stray too far from my roots, so the majority of the recipes here are Chinese classics or updated versions of traditional Chinese dishes. Wherever possible, I have re-examined the ingredients and cooking methods to see if we can trim off a few more calories here, add a little fiber there. You will find some non-Chinese ingredients used in a very Chinese way, such as ground turkey in place of pork in *dim sum* stuffings, and brown rice in vegetable fried rice.

For those who are short on time (and who isn't nowadays?) I am always looking for ways to save time in the kitchen. Many of the recipes can take advantage of those two marvelous timesavers of the modern kitchen, the food processor and the microwave oven, which have earned themselves an important place in my kitchen alongside the wok, the steamer, and other traditional Chinese cooking utensils.

To the many faithful readers and viewers who have watched me and wokked with me over the years, as well as all the new members of the audience who are enjoying their first wok, I wish you new joy and great health. Remember, if Yan Can Cook, so can you!

The Basics

Timeless Cooking for Time-less Cooks

Fads come and go, but the basic truths never change. People want to eat good-tasting food, and they need to eat nutritious, well-balanced meals. What's more, they don't want to spend an excessive amount of time preparing everyday meals. But saving time in the kitchen doesn't have to mean buying a lot of prepackaged, heavily processed, expensive "convenience" foods. Instead of looking to the newest technology, why not look back to some of the oldest?

Chinese cooks figured out thousands of years ago how to provide a balanced, healthful diet to a large number of people living in a crowded land with limited resources. Nobody wanted to spend all day cooking back then either; there was other work to do. (Sound familiar?) In the process, they developed a style of cooking that is as up-to-date as today's headlines.

There are no great mysteries to Chinese cooking. The few basic cutting techniques are easily mastered. The basic cooking equipment is found in most kitchens (you don't even really need a wok—a large skillet will do for stir-frying, though a wok is more efficient). Of the fundamental cooking methods, only two, stir-frying and steaming, are not already familiar to most cooks, and these are easy to learn. The other basic techniques, including simmering, broiling, roasting, deep-frying, and pan-frying, are well known to cooks throughout the world.

The wok is the perfect symbol of this timeless but modern cuisine. This simple, versatile cooking utensil, which has hardly changed in design in more than a thousand years, is a marvel of efficiency. With slight variations in shape and materials, it is found not only in China, but all over East Asia from Korea to India and Indonesia. Its round-bottomed shape cooks food quickly over concentrated heat. This quick cooking preserves the flavor, texture, and nutritional value of the food better than any other method. Cutting up the food into small pieces not only saves cooking time, it saves energy. This is not something we think about a lot in our modern Western kitchens with gas or electric stoves, but as the world grows more crowded, we can all do our part to make our energy resources go farther.

The ancients can teach us a thing or two about health as well. Your wok is not only a time-saver, it may also be a life-saver. Western doctors have finally realized that the traditional Asian diet is more healthful than that of the industrialized West. Heart disease and colon, breast, and lung cancers, all major killers in North America, are much less common in China, and among Chinese living here who follow a traditional lifestyle. The reason appears to be largely diet. In one study, the typical Chinese diet was shown to get less than 15 percent of its calories from fat, compared to 38 to 40 percent in the West. The overall amount of protein in the Chinese diet is two-thirds what it is in the West, and the vast majority of that protein comes from plant sources rather than animal foods.

Nobody expects that North Americans will change their eating habits overnight to the Chinese style. But more and more people are trying to cut down on fat and meat and get more of their daily calories from vegetables and grains. The recipes in this book offer plenty of delicious evidence that Chinese and other Asian foods can be part of a healthier lifestyle for all of us.

But all this talk about food is making me hungry. Let's get into the kitchen and start cooking!

Getting Organized

Organization is the key to all good cooking, East or West. If you are well organized in your menu planning and in the preparation of each dish, cooking a meal can be wonderfully satisfying. A lack of organization, on the other hand, can cause frustration.

The first step in getting organized is to decide which dishes will make up your meal. A quick and simple Asian-style menu might consist of just rice and one stir-fried or braised dish that combines some vegetables with meat, poultry, or seafood. If you want to serve a more elaborate meal, a good selection would be one braised dish, a steamed dish (which also cooks without much attention), and one or at most two stir-fried dishes. You can finish cooking the braised dish in the oven to give yourself more space on the stovetop. Consider also some of the cold dishes in the Vegetables and Salads chapter, most of which can be prepared a couple of hours in advance.

There are no hard and fast rules for creating Asian-style menus; stick to foods you like that are in season and you can't really go wrong. When choosing ingredients, a Chinese cook thinks about a variety of colors and textures as well as flavors. A meal of all soft, soupy dishes or all bright red dishes will become monotonous even if the flavors are quite varied. It's better to find some contrast—set off a tender braised dish with a dish of crunchy green vegetables, for example.

Once you have settled on the recipes you're going to cook, assemble all the ingredients, tools, and dishes you will need. If you find unfamiliar ingredients in a recipe, consult the Glossary at the end of the book for information on buying, storing, and cooking. Check the recipes for ingredients that need soaking, marinating, or other advance preparation. While those ingredients are soaking, you can prepare other ingredients or start on other dishes in the meal. Some recipes have groups of ingredients that can be combined ahead of time—sauce liquids, for instance, or minced ginger and garlic for stir-frying. If you're going to stir-fry, set out a bowl or plate ready to hold cooked or partially cooked foods that have to be removed from the wok and put back in later.

Chinese cooking is naturally fast food. More than half of the dishes in this book can be prepared in about the time it takes to cook a pot of rice. For days when even that is too much time, choose recipes with sauces that can be made ahead. Take a few spare minutes on a weeknight or on the weekend to make one or more sauces and refrigerate them; then, on a busy night later in the week, you can whip up a delicious stir-fried dish even faster than usual. Make-ahead sauces will keep for a couple of weeks tightly sealed in a jar in the refrigerator.

Some of the most popular make-ahead Chinese sauces are the fragrant Master Sauce on page 105; the zesty, chile-flavored Kung Pao Sauce on page 45; the subtle, velvety Clear Stir-Fry Sauce on page 120; and the ever-popular Sweet and Sour Sauce on page 70.

Another time-saving technique is to cook more than one dish in the same pan. For example, after cooking a teriyaki steak in a skillet, you can use the same pan to stir-fry an assortment of vegetables. Heat the teriyaki sauce in a small saucepan on the side and you have an easy meal (see page 102). Or poach chicken wings in lightly seasoned broth, then add shredded lettuce to the broth for a simple but delicious soup (see page 37).

Basic Tools

On her first trip to the United States nothing impressed my mother more than the modern American kitchen. The automatic garage door opener was great fun but it could not possibly compare to my food processor and microwave oven. Like my mother, you can be an excellent Chinese cook with very few tools and utensils. Most Chinese dishes can be prepared as they have been for thousands of years—with just a wok, a steamer, a Chinese chef's knife, and a cutting board. But many Chinese dishes benefit from non-traditional methods and tools. The long-trusted wok and bamboo steamer work well side by side with state-of-the-art kitchen gadgets.

The Wok

Think of your wok as a multi-purpose pan, not just a pan for stir-frying. With the wok you can steam, braise, and deep-fry, make soups, even pop corn. Like fine musical instruments different woks have different qualities. I have several woks at home, a few that I inherited from my mother and others I bought in this country. Some are round-bottomed, the traditional and most efficient shape; others have a flat bottom, a recent invention designed for electric stoves.

Woks of spun carbon steel, the most common type, are a good choice. They conduct heat evenly, retain high temperatures, and are reasonably priced. If you select a carbon steel wok, you will need to "season" it before you use it. First, scour the wok with hot, soapy water to remove any protective coating applied at the factory. Then dry it thoroughly, rub vegetable oil evenly into the cooking surface, and heat until the inner surface turns brown. This builds the first layer of a "seasoned" surface that keeps food from sticking during cooking. After each use, wash the wok with hot water (use very little or no soap), dry it well, and rub in a bit of fresh oil.

Woks are also made of stainless steel, often aluminum- or copper-clad for efficient heat conduction. Anodized aluminum woks with nonstick surfaces are also available. They require no seasoning, are scratch-resistant, and don't react with food. If you're concerned about lowering calories and fat, choose a wok with a nonstick cooking surface.

Another option is a good quality electric wok. It will give you constant heat control, and freedom and flexibility in a variety of preparations. It's like a portable stove. If you do purchase an electric wok, get one with at least 1500 watts of power to have enough heat for Chinese-style cooking.

If you are shopping for a new wok, be sure to get one with a lid. Many woks come in sets which also include a curved spatula, which is ideal for stirring and scraping up the contents of the salad-bowl-shaped wok; a wire skimmer, for retrieving and draining fried or boiled foods; and a pair of bamboo cooking chopsticks. (If not included, these tools are available separately.)

Longer and thicker than the chopsticks used at the table, cooking chopsticks are handy for a lot of kitchen jobs. I use them when deep-frying or boiling, to move the food around without getting my hands too close to the hot oil or water. They're also great for stirring and blending liquid ingredients and batters.

The Steamer

The Chinese have been "letting off steam" in the kitchen for thousands of years. Steaming is an ancient but very modern cooking style. It's a wonderfully healthy, low-fat way to prepare meats, fish, and vegetables. The food cooks in its own juices, retaining all its natural goodness. No wonder it's the most popular technique in Chinese home cooking.

Many Chinese homemakers prefer traditional bamboo steamers because their woven tops allow excess steam to escape without condensing and dripping back into the food. Best of all, they're stackable — more guests, more dishes, more layers.

If you don't have a bamboo steamer set, don't panic. You can still steam. Use small cans, such as tuna or water chestnut cans, with the tops and bottoms removed as stands to hold heatproof dishes above simmering water in a wok or other large pan. Or, do it the old-fashioned Chinese way: cross two pairs of chopsticks in a tic-tac-toe pattern to make a stand for the dish.

The Chinese Chef's Knife

To keep fit, I exercise every day with my Chinese chef's knife. I use it to chop, slice, dice, and mince, not to mention smash and tenderize. It is without a doubt my best friend in the kitchen. The basic design of this essential tool, with its broad rectangular blade and slightly curved edge, has hardly changed in centuries. A good Chinese knife is well balanced, feels good in the hand, is easy to sharpen, and keeps its edge well. Ideally, it should be made of high carbon stainless steel,

13

so the metal of the blade does not react with onions, garlic, or acid foods. (For years I was unable to find a stainless steel Chinese chef's knife to my liking, so I designed my own. It's the one I always use on the Yan Can Cook show, and my mother likes it too. The knife is available nationwide in select stores. If you can't find it, write to us at P.O. Box 4755, Foster City, CA 94404.)

In addition to the basic cutting tasks illustrated on page 16, you can use the flat side of the blade to crush garlic cloves or slices of ginger or to pound thinly sliced meats even thinner. You can pound tough cuts of meat with the back edge of the blade to tenderize them.

A good cutting surface is essential. A hardwood cutting board or a traditional Chinese round chopping block is easiest on your knife's edge. White plastic cutting boards are also fine. They can be washed easily, even in the dishwasher, and do not easily absorb odors from foods. Look for one that has some give to it. Those with a hard, shiny surface can be hard on your knife's edge, and are downright dangerous if the knife slips.

Ovens and Broilers

According to my mother, the oven is the most interesting gadget in an American kitchen. There is no oven in a traditional Chinese home kitchen; roasted meats and fowl are bought from carry-out shops where many are roasted at once in large ovens. Nevertheless, you can make a startling variety of Chinese dishes in your traditional or convection oven—barbecued pork, spareribs, even the famous Peking duck. In addition, you can use the oven for many casseroles, stews, and braised dishes traditionally cooked on top of the stove. This can be especially handy when you are preparing a meal of several courses and want to have more burners free on the stove top, or whenever you want to cook something slowly without a lot of attention. Many Asian dishes that are normally grilled over an open fire can also be cooked under a home broiler.

14

The Microwave Oven

A microwave oven won't replace your wok or conventional oven, but it can make it easier to prepare many dishes. It defrosts pieces of frozen meat in minutes (if the meat is to be sliced, thaw it only half-way for easier slicing). Leftover rice, noodles, and stir-fried dishes reheat well in the microwave. You can also cook a variety of Chinese dishes in the microwave, including soups, steamed dishes, and casseroles.

The Food Processor

No matter how swift you are with a cleaver (and I dare say that I am pretty handy with one), you cannot beat the convenience of a food processor. For one thing, it never gets tired, even if you have to chop vegetables for a banquet of 150.

A food processor offers shortcuts not only for chopping vegetables, but also for chopping and mincing such ingredients as garlic, ginger, and meat. The trick is to use the pulse button to get finely minced, not pulverized, ingredients. The food processor also is superb for slicing firm vegetables and for kneading dough for a variety of dim sum and Chinese dumplings.

The Rice Cooker

If you cook rice anywhere near as often as most Asian families do, an electric rice cooker is a good investment. It produces perfect rice every time, and it frees a burner on the stove for other things. Look for one with a "keep warm" setting.

Basic Techniques

Cutting

The basic cutting techniques used in Chinese cooking are illustrated on page 16.

Marinating

Many Asian recipes call for marinating meats, poultry, and seafood before cooking. The marinating is mainly to add flavor, not to tenderize the food. About

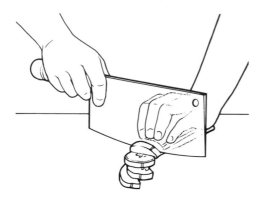

Holding the knife: Note that the fingertips of the left hand are held vertically.

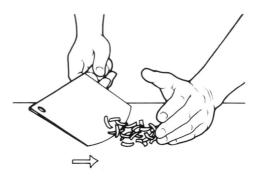

Transferring food: The Chinese Chef's knife is an ideal tool for gathering up cut ingredients.

Slicing, shown here with lotus root.

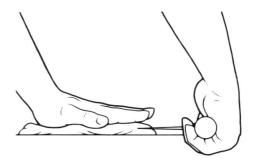

Horizontal slicing, to reduce the thickness of an ingredient. Keep fingertips up out of the way.

Dicing: Make horizontal cuts, then vertical; slice across both cuts. *To mince,* make all cuts closer together.

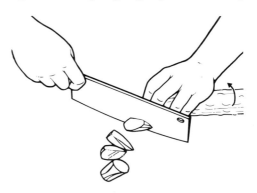

Roll-cutting: A nice alternative for cylindrical vegetables. Slice at an angle, then roll the vegetable a quarter turn.

30 minutes of marinating is plenty in most cases, but you can also marinate foods ahead of time and refrigerate them in the marinade until ready to cook. Some recipes say to drain the food or lift it out of the marinade. Otherwise, small amounts of marinade can go into the wok along with the meat; they will evaporate quickly and add flavor to the finished dish.

Microwaving

Where appropriate, I have noted ways to use your microwave oven to save time or cleanup steps.

When the directions indicate a covered dish, leave the lid slightly ajar or cover the dish with plastic wrap, cutting a small opening for the steam to escape.

The microwave can reduce the time needed for soaking dried black mushrooms and other dried ingredients. Place up to six black mushrooms in a 1-quart microwave-safe bowl, cover, and cook on high for 5 minutes; then let stand until soft, about 5 minutes.

Soaking

Asian cuisines use many dried ingredients such as black mushrooms, tangerine peel, and shrimp, all of which need to be soaked for about 30 minutes before they are ready to use. If you start them soaking first thing, before you begin cooking the rice or washing, cutting up, and marinating the other ingredients, they will be ready when you need them. If you know you will be short on time, soak and drain the necessary ingredients the night before and refrigerate them.

Toasting

To bring out the flavor in Sichuan peppercorns or sesame seeds, place them in a small dry skillet and cook them over medium heat, shaking the pan frequently, until they are slightly darkened and very aromatic. Small quantities of nuts can also be toasted this way; spread larger quantities of nuts on a baking sheet and toast them in a 350° oven until golden brown.

17

Appetizers and Soups

Shrimp with Orange-Mustard Sauce
Bell Peppers Stuffed with Seafood Mousse
Thai Pork and Shrimp Toasts
Filipino Lumpia
Chilled Fish, Shanghai Style
Glazed Sichuan Chicken Wings
Chiu Chow Dumplings
Skewered Chicken with Sesame Dip
Marbled Tea Eggs
Fresh Vietnamese Rice Paper Bundles
Dim Sum Turkey Balls
Chicken Coconut Soup
Fish, Spinach, and Tofu Soup
Dried Bok Choy Soup
Lettuce Soup with Poached Chicken Wings
Corn and Shellfish Soup
Wor Wonton Soup
Hot and Sour Shrimp Soup

Appetizers

Appetizers, in the Western sense of the word, are uncommon in China. We like to get right down to serious eating! But everyday meals in some parts of China include a few little dishes that complement the rest of the meal. Many of these little dishes make delightful appetizers in a Western-style menu. Here are some of my favorites, including a few examples of the Cantonese teahouse tidbits known as *dim sum*. Of course, most of the appetizer recipes in this chapter can serve fewer people as a "main" dish.

Shrimp with Orange-Mustard Sauce

Simply wonderful! I love the combination of orange and mustard. Although traditional Chinese kitchens don't have ovens, this updated recipe is baked. Still it has all the elements of the traditional Chinese dish, which is "dry-fried" in a wok.

Makes about 20

1. Combine the marinade ingredients in a medium bowl. Add the shrimp; stir to coat. Set aside for 20 minutes. Combine the sauce ingredients in a small serving bowl; set aside.

2. Preheat the oven to 400°. Place the shrimp on a rack in a foil-lined baking pan. Bake until the shrimp feel firm and turn pink, about 6 minutes. Arrange on a platter. Serve warm or at room temperature with the dipping sauce.

TIP: Check the shrimp a minute or two before the recommended baking time is up; it is important not to overcook the shrimp.

Marinade
1 tablespoon soy sauce
1 tablespoon dry sherry or
   Chinese rice wine
1 teaspoon sesame oil
1 teaspoon vegetable oil
1 teaspoon grated
   orange peel
1 teaspoon cornstarch

❀

1 pound (20 to 30) large or
   medium raw shrimp,
   shelled and deveined with
   tail shells left on

Dipping Sauce
2 tablespoons fresh lime juice
3 tablespoons soy sauce
3 tablespoons orange
   marmalade
2 teaspoons prepared
   Chinese mustard

Bell Peppers Stuffed with Seafood Mousse

Fish Mousse

2 dried black mushrooms
¼ pound white fish fillet
   (sole, snapper, or lingcod)
¼ pound raw shrimp,
   shelled and deveined
1 egg white
1½ teaspoons sesame oil
1 tablespoon chicken broth
1 teaspoon cornstarch
⅛ teaspoon white pepper

✿

2 green bell peppers,
   seeded and cut into
   about 2-inch squares
Cornstarch for dry-coating
4 tablespoons vegetable oil
¾ cup chicken broth
2 teaspoons minced garlic
1 teaspoon minced ginger
1 teaspoon chopped shallots
½ teaspoon crushed
   red pepper
3 tablespoons Chinese
   preserved black beans,
   rinsed, drained, and
   coarsely chopped
2 tablespoons dry sherry
1 tablespoon soy sauce
1 teaspoon sugar
1½ teaspoons cornstarch
   dissolved in
   1 tablespoon water

My food processor makes the seafood mousse for these stuffed bell pepper squares in no time. I cook the stuffed peppers in a regular wide frying pan and serve them with black bean sauce. They make nice appetizers as well as dim sum offerings.

Makes 16

1. Soak the mushrooms in warm water to cover for 30 minutes; drain. Cut off and discard the stems; cut the caps into quarters. Place the mushrooms in a food processor and process until finely chopped. Add the remaining mousse ingredients and process to a smooth paste.

2. Lightly dust the inside of the bell pepper squares with cornstarch. Spread about 2 teaspoons of mousse on each square. (The squares can be prepared to this point up to 2 hours ahead of time and refrigerated.)

3. Place a wide frying pan over medium-high heat. Add 1 tablespoon of the vegetable oil, swirling to coat the surface. Place half the stuffed peppers in the pan filling side down and cook for 1½ minutes. Add ¼ cup of broth; cover and cook until the peppers are tender, about 3 minutes. Remove the peppers from the pan and keep them warm. Wipe the pan dry and cook the remaining peppers with another tablespoon of oil and ¼ cup of broth.

4. Meanwhile, place a small saucepan over high heat. Add the remaining 2 tablespoons of vegetable oil, swirling to coat the surface. Add the garlic, ginger, shallots, and red pepper and cook for 30 seconds. Add the black beans, sherry, soy sauce, sugar, and the remaining broth; mix well. Add the cornstarch solution and cook, stirring, until the sauce boils and thickens. Spoon the sauce over the stuffed peppers.

VARIATION: For a different flavor, stuff fresh Anaheim green chiles. Cut the peppers in half lengthwise; remove the seeds and veins before cutting into squares for stuffing.

Thai Pork and Shrimp Toasts

12 slices firm,
   day-old white bread

Pork and Shrimp Paste
¼ pound lean ground pork
¼ pound medium raw shrimp,
   shelled and deveined
 1 tablespoon chopped green
   onion (including top)
 1 serrano or jalapeño chile,
   minced
 2 egg whites
 2 teaspoons chopped cilantro
   (Chinese
   parsley) roots and
   1 inch of stems
 1 teaspoon chopped
   cilantro leaves
 1 teaspoon minced garlic
 ½ teaspoon salt
 ⅛ teaspoon black pepper
   ✿
Vegetable oil for deep-frying
Cilantro leaves for garnish

I can't understand why the Thais are the only ones who cook with cilantro roots. The roots have a deep, rich flavor, less spicy than the feathery leaves. My produce man is so fastidious he trims off the roots, so I save a spot in my garden to grow my own supply. You can omit the roots from this recipe; the toast will still taste great, just not quite as authentically Thai.

Makes 24

1. Trim the crusts from the bread and cut each slice in half diagonally.

2. In a food processor, combine the paste ingredients and process to make a coarse paste. Spread the paste about ¼ inch thick on one side of each bread triangle. If you wish, you may place the triangles in a single layer in a baking pan and cover and refrigerate them for up to 2 hours.

3. Set a wok in a ring stand and add oil to a depth of about 2 inches. Heat over medium-high heat until the oil reaches 360°. Add the triangles paste side down, a few at a time; cook for 1½ minutes. Turn them and cook until golden brown, about 30 seconds. The edges will be curled like furled ribbon. Lift the toasts out and drain them on paper towels. Keep them warm in a 200° oven while cooking the rest. Arrange the toasts on a flat basket and garnish them with cilantro leaves. Serve hot.

TIPS: The toasts are large—hearty enough for a snack. For a party appetizer, cut each slice of bread into 4 triangles or cut it into circles with a 2-inch cookie cutter. You can also try thinly sliced French bread.

Leftover cilantro roots can be frozen for later use.

Filipino Lumpia

Dipping Sauce
2 teaspoons minced garlic
¼ cup chicken broth
2 tablespoons soy sauce
2 tablespoons rice vinegar
¼ cup (packed) brown sugar
2 tablespoons cornstarch
   dissolved in 2 tablespoons
   water

Filling
1 Chinese sausage
   (about 2 ounces)
1 medium russet potato
1 small carrot
4 ounces jicama
2 tablespoons vegetable oil
1 tablespoon minced garlic
1 teaspoon minced ginger
½ pound lean ground pork
1 cup shredded
   Chinese (napa) cabbage
1 small chayote,
   peeled and shredded
3 green onions
   (including tops), slivered
2 tablespoons chicken broth,
   if needed
2 tablespoons soy sauce
1 tablespoon dry sherry or
   Chinese rice wine
1 teaspoon sesame oil
1 teaspoon cornstarch
   dissolved in 2 teaspoons
   water
❀
8 spring roll wrappers or
   lumpia wrappers
1 egg, lightly beaten
Oil for deep-frying
8 lettuce leaves for garnish

Many Southeast Asian countries enjoy variations of the Chinese egg roll; Lumpia is the delicate Filipino version. Lumpia wrappers are thinner than egg roll wrappers. You can purchase them, frozen, in Asian markets.

Makes 8

1. Combine the dipping sauce ingredients (except the cornstarch solution) in a small saucepan and bring to a boil over medium-high heat. Add the cornstarch solution and cook, stirring, until the sauce boils and thickens. Remove from the heat.

2. Cut the sausage, potato, carrot, and jicama into match-stick pieces. Place a wok or wide frying pan over medium-high heat until hot. Add 2 tablespoons of oil, swirling to coat the sides of the pan. Add the garlic and ginger and cook, stirring, until fragrant, about 10 seconds. Add the pork, sausage, and potato and stir-fry until the pork is browned and crumbly and the potato is soft, 3 to 4 minutes. Add the cabbage, chayote, carrot, jicama, and green onions; stir-fry until the carrot is crisp-tender, about 2 minutes. Add broth if the mixture becomes too dry. Stir in the soy sauce, sherry, and sesame oil and add the cornstarch solution. Cook, stirring, until the sauce boils and thickens. Transfer the filling to a bowl and refrigerate until cool.

3. Lay a wrapper on the table with one corner toward you; keep the remaining wrappers covered to prevent drying. Mound about ⅓ cup of filling across the middle of the wrapper, stopping 1 inch from the corners. Fold the bottom corner over the filling to cover, then fold over the right and left corners. Roll over once to enclose the filling. Brush the remaining triangle of the wrapper with egg and fold over to seal. Cover the filled lumpia with a damp cloth while filling the remaining wrappers.

4. Heat the oven to 200°. Set a wok in a ring stand and add vegetable oil to a depth of about 2 inches. Heat the oil to 360°; adjust the heat to medium-high. Fry

the lumpia, half at a time, turning occasionally, until golden brown, 2 to 3 minutes. Keep the fried rolls warm in the oven while cooking the remaining rolls. Meanwhile, reheat the dipping sauce. Serve the lumpia on a platter lined with lettuce leaves. Serve the dipping sauce alongside.

Chilled Fish, Shanghai Style

1 pound fillets of
   firm-textured white fish,
   such as cod or halibut,
   about ¾ inch thick

Marinade
1 teaspoon minced garlic
1 teaspoon minced ginger
3 tablespoons soy sauce
3 tablespoons dry sherry or
   Chinese rice wine
1 tablespoon (packed)
   brown sugar
¼ teaspoon Chinese five-spice
❀
Lettuce leaves for garnish

Shanghai cuisine is known for its richly marinated seafood, served chilled or at room temperature. This contemporary recipe is similar to a smoked fish appetizer popular in Shanghai restaurants. Usually deep-fried, it's just as delicious broiled.

Serves 4

1. Score the fish with shallow parallel cuts at 1-inch intervals. Make another set of cuts at an angle to the first to make a diamond pattern. Combine the marinade ingredients in a shallow dish. Add the fish, turning it to coat both sides. Cover and refrigerate for at least 1 hour or overnight.

2. Remove the fish from the marinade and place it on a rack in a foil-lined baking pan; reserve the marinade. Broil the fish 2 to 3 inches from the heat until opaque in the center, about 6 minutes. Transfer it to a deep plate; set aside.

3. Pour the reserved marinade into a small saucepan. Bring it to a boil over medium-high heat and boil for 2 minutes. Strain the liquid over the fish and let it stand for 30 minutes. Pour off and discard the marinade; cover and refrigerate the fish until ready to serve. Serve on a bed of lettuce leaves.

TIP: Try serving the fish with Belgian endive leaves as part of an appetizer plate.

Glazed Sichuan Chicken Wings

12 whole chicken wings

Marinade
1 tablespoon soy sauce
1 tablespoon dry sherry or
  Chinese rice wine
Pinch of white pepper

Seasoning Mixture
4 thin slices ginger, crushed
1 green onion
  (including top), halved
½ teaspoon toasted
  Sichuan peppercorns
  (page 17)
½ teaspoon crushed
  red pepper

✿

2 tablespoons vegetable oil
2 whole dried chile peppers
¼ cup chicken broth
2 tablespoons dark soy sauce
2 tablespoons dry sherry or
  Chinese rice wine
4 teaspoons (packed)
  dark brown sugar
1½ teaspoons cornstarch
  dissolved in 1 tablespoon
  water

These chicken wings are hot stuff! The peppery sauce can be used again and again to simmer meats and poultry—it only gets more flavorful with each use. Just strain after using and refrigerate or freeze until you're ready to cook with it again.

Makes 24

1. Separate the chicken wings into sections; discard the bony tips. Combine the marinade ingredients in a medium bowl. Add the chicken wings. Stir to coat and set aside for 30 minutes. Combine the seasoning mixture ingredients in a small bowl; set aside.

2. Place a wok or wide frying pan over high heat until hot. Add the oil and whole chiles, swirling to coat the sides of the pan. Add the chicken wings; cook, stirring, until golden brown, about 3 minutes. Add the seasoning mixture; stir for 15 seconds. Stir in the broth, dark soy sauce, sherry, and sugar. Bring to a boil; reduce the heat, cover, and simmer until the chicken wings are tender when pierced, about 12 minutes.

3. Remove and discard the chiles, ginger, and green onion. Increase the heat to high. Add the cornstarch solution; cook, stirring, until the sauce boils and thickens and the wings are glazed, about 2 minutes.

TIP: Stand back a bit from your wok when stir-frying chiles. The volatile oils released by the chiles may sting your nose and eyes.

Chiu Chow Dumplings

Dough

1 ⅓ cups wheat starch
1 tablespoon cornstarch
⅔ cup boiling water
1 teaspoon lard

Filling

2 tablespoons dried shrimp, soaked (see page 17) and coarsely chopped
½ pound lean pork, coarsely chopped or ground
¼ cup coarsely chopped walnuts or unsalted peanuts
1 tablespoon chopped cilantro (Chinese parsley)
1 teaspoon minced ginger
2 tablespoons chicken broth or water
1 tablespoon soy sauce
1 tablespoon dry sherry or Chinese rice wine
2 teaspoons sesame oil
Pinch of white pepper
2 teaspoons cornstarch

✿

Soy sauce
Prepared Chinese mustard

These delicious dumplings with their transparent skins come from the Chiu Chow cuisine, named after a region around Shantou in southeastern China. Chiu Chow dishes and restaurants are common in Hong Kong and most of the cities of Southeast Asia, where people from this region have settled as emigrants and traders for centuries.

Makes about 30

1. Combine the wheat starch and cornstarch in a bowl. Add the boiling water, stirring with chopsticks or a fork until the dough is evenly moistened. Cover and let rest for 20 minutes. Combine the filling ingredients in a bowl. Cover and refrigerate until ready to use.

2. On a lightly oiled surface, knead the dough until smooth. Work in the lard, ¼ teaspoon at a time, kneading after each addition until the dough glistens and feels satiny. Divide the dough in half. Roll each half into a 15-inch-long cylinder. Cut each cylinder crosswise into 1-inch pieces; shape each piece into a ball. Cover with a damp cloth to prevent drying.

3. Flatten a ball of dough and roll with a rolling pin into a 3-inch circle. Spoon 1 heaping teaspoon of filling in the center of the circle. Lightly moisten the edges with water and fold the circle in half. Starting at one end, seal the curved edges together with 4 to 6 pleats, pinching the edges to seal securely. Cover the filled dumplings with a damp cloth while shaping the rest.

4. Line the bottoms of two bamboo steamers with small damp cloths. Arrange half the dumplings in each without crowding. Bring 2 inches of water to a boil in a wok. Stack the steamers, cover, and steam over boiling water until the dumplings are translucent, 10 to 12 minutes. Serve with soy sauce and mustard.

TIP: Wheat starch, the starchy part of flour separated from the gluten, is a pure white powder with the look and feel of cornstarch. It is sold in Chinese groceries.

Skewered Chicken with Sesame Dip

Marinade
2 teaspoons minced garlic
2 tablespoons soy sauce
1 tablespoon peanut butter
1 tablespoon vegetable oil
1 teaspoon chili paste

✿

1½ pounds boneless chicken breasts, skinned and cut into 1-inch-wide strips
12 short bamboo skewers

Sesame Dip
3 tablespoons sesame seeds, toasted (see page 17), or 1 tablespoon sesame paste
1 teaspoon minced garlic
1 egg yolk
2 tablespoons rice vinegar
1 tablespoon honey
½ teaspoon chili paste
½ teaspoon crushed red pepper
¼ teaspoon salt
1 teaspoon sesame oil
½ cup vegetable oil

✿

½ cup dried bread crumbs

Most of the time I cook with Chinese ingredients, but I don't mind borrowing Western cooking styles. In this case, I've made a sesame dip with the same technique used to make mayonnaise. The sauce is creamy and aromatic, perfect for grilled chicken bits. I think you'll like this East-West blend.

Serves 12

1. Combine the marinade ingredients in a medium bowl. Add the chicken and stir to coat. Set aside for 30 minutes. Soak the skewers in water for 30 minutes.

2. In a blender or food processor, combine the sesame seeds, garlic, egg yolk, vinegar, honey, chili paste, red pepper, and salt. Add the sesame oil and process until well blended. With the motor running, add the vegetable oil, a few drops at first then increasing to a slow steady trickle, until the mixture thickens. Transfer the dip to a bowl. Cover and refrigerate for at least 30 minutes for flavors to blend.

3. Weave the chicken strips lengthwise on the skewers and roll them in bread crumbs. Place them on a rack in a foil-lined baking pan and broil 2 to 3 inches below the heat (or grill 3 to 4 inches above a solid bed of low-glowing coals). Cook, turning to brown all sides, until the chicken is no longer pink when pierced, 8 to 10 minutes. Serve with sesame dip.

TIPS: Panko, coarse Japanese-style bread crumbs, give a great crispy finish to the chicken. If you cannot find panko, process dried sweet French bread in the food processor to make coarse crumbs.

This dish is also wonderful as an entree; it will serve 6.

Marbled Tea Eggs

8 eggs
1 green onion
  (including top), crushed
1 teaspoon slivered ginger
¼ cup regular soy sauce
¼ cup dark soy sauce
3 tablespoons black
  tea leaves
2 tablespoons (packed)
  dark brown sugar
½ teaspoon Chinese five-spice
3 whole star anise
1 cinnamon stick

These fragrant, distinctively colored eggs, "marbled" with a mixture of tea and soy sauce, are popular as an appetizer or a between-meal snack in eastern China. Even at midnight, you can hear Shanghai street vendors calling "Marble egg! Marble egg!" They are equally good day or night.

Makes 8

1. Place the eggs in a medium saucepan; cover with cold water. Bring to a boil, reduce the heat, and simmer for 10 minutes. Cool the eggs under cold running water and drain. Gently tap each egg all over with a spoon until hairline cracks form over the entire shell.

2. While the eggs are cooking, bring the remaining ingredients to a boil in a medium saucepan. Reduce the heat to a gentle boil, cover, and cook for 15 minutes.

3. Place the cooked eggs into the soy mixture, adding extra water if necessary to cover the eggs. Simmer, covered, over low heat for 1 hour. Remove the pan from the heat; let the eggs cool in the liquid, then refrigerate (still in the liquid) overnight or for up to 2 days. Peel the eggs just before serving and place in a serving bowl.

TIPS: Use a fresh batch of tea leaves for this recipe; old tea leaves will not release as much flavor.

The combination of regular and dark soy sauces provides a balance of colors and flavors neither sauce can give on its own.

Fresh Vietnamese Rice Paper Bundles

Dipping Sauce
1 teaspoon minced garlic
3 tablespoons rice vinegar
2 tablespoons lime juice
2 tablespoons fish sauce
2 teaspoons chili paste
4 teaspoons sugar

❀

3 cups shredded
   cooked chicken
1 tablespoon fish sauce
1 teaspoon sesame oil
1 teaspoon chopped cilantro
   (Chinese parsley),
   plus 12 sprigs
Pinch of black pepper
12 dried 7-inch
   rice paper rounds
2 ounces bean threads,
   soaked, drained, and cut
   into 3-inch lengths
1 bunch watercress,
   tough stems removed
½ red bell pepper,
   seeded and cut into
   matchstick pieces
3 green onions
   (including tops), slivered
Mint leaves for garnish

If Vietnam had a national dish, it would be this popular variation of the spring roll. The delicious *cha gio* are wrapped in phyllo-thin rice paper wrappers that have been carefully softened with water or other liquid before rolling.

Makes 12

1. Combine the dipping sauce ingredients in a small serving bowl and stir until the sugar dissolves. Set aside. Combine the chicken, fish sauce, sesame oil, chopped cilantro, and black pepper in a medium bowl.

2. To assemble each bundle, immerse a rice paper round in cool water for about 10 seconds then transfer it to a flat working surface. Let it stand for 1 minute or until it becomes soft and pliable. Place about ¼ cup of the chicken mixture in the center and top with a small mound of bean threads, 2 or 3 pieces each of watercress, bell pepper, and green onion, and a cilantro sprig. Roll the wrapper around the filling, tucking in one end. Serve the bundles on a platter, garnished with mint leaves. Offer dipping sauce at the table.

TIP: If all you can find are 9- or 12-inch rice paper rounds, make larger bundles and cut them into thirds before serving.

Dim Sum Turkey Balls

One 2-inch strip dried
tangerine peel OR
2 tablespoons finely
chopped fresh orange
or tangerine peel
1 pound ground turkey
½ cup finely chopped
water chestnuts
1 tablespoon chopped cilantro
(Chinese parsley)
2 tablespoons chicken broth
or water
2 tablespoons oyster sauce
1 tablespoon soy sauce
2 teaspoons sesame oil
2 tablespoons cornstarch

✿

1 large bunch watercress,
blanched, for garnish
Worcestershire sauce OR
soy sauce mixed with
prepared Chinese mustard
to taste, for dipping

I've given this dim sum item a modern twist by using ground turkey rather than the traditional beef. Lean and healthful, the turkey blends nicely with the flavor of tangerine. Terrific as dim sum or an appetizer, turkey balls are also a great main dish.

Makes 20

1. If using dried tangerine peel, soak it in warm water to cover for 30 minutes; drain and mince. Combine all the ingredients except the watercress and dipping sauce in a medium bowl; mix well. With wet hands, shape the mixture into 20 meatballs, each approximately 1½ inches in diameter.

2. Place a steaming rack in a wok; add water to just below the level of the rack and bring it to a boil. Arrange the turkey balls in two greased 9-inch glass pie pans. Set one pan on the rack, cover, and steam until the turkey is no longer pink (cut a small slit through a turkey ball to test), about 12 minutes. Serve the first portion while you steam the second. Place the watercress on a serving platter and arrange the turkey balls on top. Serve with Worcestershire sauce or the soy-mustard dip.

VARIATION: Traditionally this dish is made with beef; you can also try it with finely chopped raw shrimp or minced chicken.

MICROWAVE METHOD: Instead of steaming the turkey balls in Step 2, place them in a 9-inch microwave-safe glass pie pan, cover, and cook on high for 2 minutes. Stir, cover, and cook on medium until the turkey is no longer pink, about 4 minutes. Serve as above.

Soups

As a boy, I'd sip along with almost every meal. Sometimes we had elaborate soups for special occasions, but mostly they were simple. I remember watching as my mother would start with a light, flavorful broth, then add a few dried mushrooms, some bean curd, bits of meat or fish, and whatever vegetables she had picked up from the market. Nothing fancy—just homey, nutritious, and comforting.

Soup is traditionally not a separate course in a Chinese meal; it is sipped throughout the meal along with the other foods. However, you may prefer to serve the following soups as a first course, or as a one-dish meal.

Chicken Coconut Soup

3 cups chicken broth
Bottom 6 inches of
  1 stalk lemongrass,
  cut into 1-inch
  pieces and crushed with
  the side of a cleaver
3 thin slices ginger
1 can (14 ounces)
  coconut milk
2 tablespoons fish sauce
1 whole chicken breast,
  skinned, boned,
  and thinly sliced
½ cup canned straw
  mushrooms
3 tablespoons fresh lime juice
1 serrano or jalapeño chile,
  seeded and slivered
1 tablespoon chopped fresh
  basil

Fragrant lemongrass, creamy coconut milk, pungent fish sauce, and hot chile flavor this aromatic soup from Thailand. My version is only moderately spiced. If you want a bolder spicy Thai flavor, double the amount of lemongrass and do not remove the seeds from the chile.

Serves 4

In a large pot, bring the broth, lemongrass, and ginger to a boil. Reduce the heat to medium, add the coconut milk and fish sauce, cover, and simmer for 8 minutes. Add the chicken, mushrooms, lime juice, and chile and cook until the chicken turns opaque, about 5 minutes. Add the basil leaves just before serving. Ladle into individual soup bowls.

TIP: Although lemongrass stalks are fibrous and are used to flavor soup rather than as an ingredient to be eaten, it is customary in Thai cooking to leave them in the soup when serving. You may prefer to discard them just as you would a bay leaf.

MICROWAVE METHOD: Combine the broth, lemongrass, and ginger in a 2-quart microwave-safe casserole and cook on high for 5 minutes. Add the coconut milk, fish sauce, chicken, straw mushrooms, lime juice, and chile; cover and cook on high until the chicken is just tender, about 3 minutes. Add the basil leaves just before serving. Serve as above.

Fish, Spinach, and Tofu Soup

4 dried black mushrooms
½ bunch (about 6 ounces) spinach
½ pound fillets of firm-textured white fish such as cod, halibut, or sea bass, ½ to ¾ inch thick
⅛ teaspoon white pepper
5 cups chicken broth
1 package (about 1 pound) soft tofu, drained and cut into ½-inch cubes
2 teaspoons sesame oil

When I was growing up, my mother prepared this simple, nutritious soup almost every day. I must have eaten it half a million times—and I still love it! It's a great starter for a light family meal.

Serves 6

1. Soak the mushrooms in warm water to cover for 30 minutes; drain. Cut off and discard the stems and thinly slice the caps. Wash the spinach; discard the heavy stems. Cut the fish into ½-inch cubes; sprinkle with pepper and set aside.

2. In a large pot, bring the broth and mushrooms to a boil over medium-high heat. Add the spinach, fish, tofu, and sesame oil. Reduce the heat to medium-low and cook until the spinach is slightly wilted, about 2 minutes. Serve immediately.

TIPS: Chard or bok choy leaves may be used in place of spinach. You can use either soft or regular tofu. I personally prefer the soft because it has a wonderfully silky-smooth texture.

Dried Bok Choy Soup

3 ounces dried bok choy
4 jujubes or dried figs
1 large can (49½ ounces)
  chicken broth
4 cups water
½ pound boneless lean pork,
  cut into ¾-inch cubes
2 thin slices ginger
Salt to taste

In ancient times, bok choy was dried to preserve it until the next growing season. Today fresh bok choy is available year round, but it is also dried because cooks and diners like the unique flavor drying gives it. My mother used to blanch the surplus from our garden and hang it on the clothesline to dry. This homespun soup was one of her specialties.

Serves 8

1. Soak the bok choy in warm water to cover for 2 hours. Wash it in clean water to remove dirt around the stems. Remove the stem ends and cut the bok choy into 1½-inch pieces. If jujubes are used, soak them in warm water to cover for 30 minutes; drain.

2. In a large pot, combine the bok choy, jujubes, chicken broth, water, pork, and ginger. Bring to a boil over high heat and skim off any foam that forms on the top. Reduce the heat, cover, and simmer for 1½ hours or until the bok choy is tender. Add salt to taste before serving.

TIPS: Jujubes, also called Chinese dates, are not actually of the date family. They are small, dried, wrinkled red fruit with an apple-prune-like taste. They are imported from northern China and grown in drier sections of the western United States. They give subtle sweetness to soups and braised dishes.

In some Chinese markets, packages of dried bok choy are labeled "dehydrated cole."

Lettuce Soup with Poached Chicken Wings

12 whole chicken wings
½ head iceberg lettuce

Pepper Salt
1 tablespoon salt
¼ teaspoon ground toasted
  Sichuan peppercorns
  (see page 17)
¼ teaspoon black pepper
¼ teaspoon Chinese five-spice
❀
1 large can (49½ ounces)
  chicken broth
2 thin slices ginger, crushed
1 green onion (including
  top), lightly crushed
1 cup frozen peas, thawed
1 small carrot,
  very thinly sliced
½ teaspoon sesame oil
¼ teaspoon white pepper
¼ cup oyster sauce

I'm a firm believer in meals in minutes. In about 15 minutes, you can cook tasty chicken wings and also create a savory soup to serve alongside.

Serves 4

1. Cut each chicken wing into 3 sections; set all pieces aside. Reserve two outer lettuce leaves to garnish the serving platter. Cut the remaining lettuce into 1-inch squares; set aside.

2. Combine the pepper salt ingredients in a small frying pan. Cook over medium heat for 2 minutes or until fragrant; set aside.

3. Combine the broth, chicken wings, ginger, and green onion in a large pot and bring to a boil. Reduce the heat to medium-low, cover, and simmer until the chicken wings are tender when pierced, about 12 minutes. Lift out and transfer the chicken wings to a serving bowl; discard the wing tips. Cover and keep warm.

4. Strain the broth and discard the ginger and green onion. Return the broth to the pot and bring it to a boil. Add the peas, carrot, lettuce squares, sesame oil, and white pepper; cook for 2 minutes.

5. To serve, arrange the chicken wings on the lettuce leaves and sprinkle them with a tiny bit of pepper salt. Pass the oyster sauce as a dip. Serve the soup on the side.

TIPS: You can use any green leafy vegetable of your choice to garnish the serving platter. Sliced mushrooms would be a nice addition to the soup. Steak sauce or Worcestershire sauce can also be used as a dip.

MICROWAVE METHOD: In step 3, combine the broth, chicken wings, ginger, and green onion in a 2½-quart microwave-safe casserole; cover and cook on high for 8 minutes. Cook on medium until the chicken is tender, about 12 minutes. In step 4, combine the strained broth and vegetables and cook on high for 1 minute.

Corn and Shellfish Soup

4 dried black mushrooms
6 cups chicken broth
1 teaspoon slivered ginger
1 can (about 1 pound)
   cream-style corn
¼ pound bay scallops
¼ pound cooked crabmeat,
   flaked
½ cup frozen peas, thawed
1 teaspoon sesame oil
¼ teaspoon white pepper
4 teaspoons cornstarch
   dissolved in 2
   tablespooons water
1 egg white

Yes, China has corn. (Where do you think the cornstarch comes from?) One favorite Chinese way to use sweet corn is in luscious seafood soups. This version uses scallops and crabmeat, but feel free to use all scallops, or any other combination of shellfish you like.

Serves 6 to 8

1. Soak the mushrooms in warm water to cover for 30 minutes; drain. Cut off and discard the stems and thinly slice the caps. Set aside.

2. In a large pot, bring the broth, ginger, and mushrooms to a boil over medium-high heat. Reduce the heat to medium, add the corn, scallops, crabmeat, and peas, and cook until the scallops turn opaque, about 1 minute. Stir in the sesame oil and pepper. Add the cornstarch solution and cook, stirring, until the soup boils and thickens. Lightly beat the egg white in a bowl. Remove the pot from the heat; slowly drizzle in the egg white, stirring constantly, to form "egg flowers."

VARIATION: If bay scallops are not available, sea scallops may be substituted; cut the sea scallops into smaller slices.

Wor Wonton Soup

6 dried black mushrooms

Filling

¼ pound lean ground pork
¼ pound medium raw shrimp, shelled, deveined, and coarsely chopped
1 green onion (including top), minced
1 tablespoon soy sauce
1 tablespoon dry sherry or Chinese rice wine
1 teaspoon sesame oil
2 teaspoons cornstarch
⅛ teaspoon white pepper

❀

20 wonton wrappers
1 large can (49½ ounces) chicken broth
1 cup sliced bok choy leaves, cut into 1-inch pieces
1 cup snow peas, ends and strings removed
½ pound Chinese barbecued pork or ham, thinly sliced
1 green onion (including top), thinly sliced
Pinch of white pepper
½ teaspoon sesame oil

Every country has its chicken soup. Wonton soup, with its ravioli-like pasta, is a wonderful Chinese version. Wonton means "swallowing the clouds." With their skirt-like sides, wontons float in soup like little trailing clouds. "Wor" in Chinese means large pot or stock pot. Wor wonton means a pot of wontons with lots of goodies.

Serves 5

1. Soak the mushrooms in warm water to cover for 30 minutes; drain. Cut off and discard the stems and thinly slice the caps. Set aside. Combine the filling ingredients in a medium bowl; mix well.

2. To fill each wonton, place 1 heaping teaspoon of filling in the center of a wonton wrapper (keep the remaining wrappers covered to prevent drying). Brush the edges of the wrapper lightly with water, fold it in half over the filling to form a triangle, and press the edges firmly to seal. Place the filled wontons slightly apart on a baking sheet and cover them with a damp cloth while filling the remaining wrappers.

3. Bring the broth to a boil in a large pot over high heat. Add the mushrooms and bok choy and cook for 2 minutes. Add the wontons and cook for 3 minutes. Add the snow peas and cook for 1 minute. Ladle the wontons and broth into large individual soup bowls and garnish each serving with slices of barbecued pork and green onion. Sprinkle with pepper and sesame oil before serving.

TIPS: In Chinese restaurants the wontons are cooked separately in water so the broth will not become cloudy. Here they are cooked in the broth for convenience.

You can fill the wontons ahead of time and cover and refrigerate them for up to 8 hours. For longer storage, freeze them on a baking sheet, then transfer them to a plastic bag and return them to the freezer. Do not thaw before cooking; add 2 minutes to the cooking time.

Hot and Sour Shrimp Soup

½ pound medium raw
  shrimp
1 tablespoon vegetable oil
5 cups chicken broth
2 stalks lemongrass, cut into
  2-inch pieces and crushed
Peel of ½ lime
1 serrano or jalapeño chile,
  cut in half
½ cup canned straw
  mushrooms
2½ tablespoons fresh
  lime juice
1 tablespoon fish sauce

Garnish

2 green onions (including
  tops), thinly sliced
2 tablespoons coarsely
  chopped cilantro
  (Chinese parsley)
1½ tablespoons coarsely
  chopped mint leaves
1 serrano or jalapeño chile,
  seeded and slivered

By upbringing, I'm thrifty. If you looked in my freezer, you'd find bags of shrimp shells tucked among the bags of Chinese sausage, barbecued pork, and noodles. I save the shells every time I clean shrimp, because they give a fresh-from-the-sea flavor to fish stock; they're essential to this fragrant Thai soup.

Serves 4

1. Shell the shrimp, rinse the shells, and pat them dry. Cut the shrimp in half horizontally and rinse out the sand veins.

2. Place a large pot over high heat until hot. Add the oil, swirling to coat the surface. Add the shrimp shells; cook until they turn pink, about 30 seconds. Add the broth, lemongrass, lime peel, and chile. Bring to a boil over high heat. Reduce the heat to medium-low, cover, and simmer for 20 minutes. Strain the broth, discarding the seasonings. Return the broth to the pot and heat to simmering. Add the shrimp and straw mushrooms and cook until the shrimp turn pink, about 2 minutes. Stir in the lime juice and fish sauce. To serve, ladle into individual soup bowls. Garnish with green onion, cilantro, mint leaves, and chile.

TIP: If you want to grow your own lemongrass, root several fresh stalks in a jar of water, just as you would a geranium cutting. Plant them in a large pot, leaving room for them to spread. They can stand light frosts, but not cold winters.

MICROWAVE METHOD: In step 2, combine the oil and shrimp shells in a 2½-quart microwave-safe casserole and cook on high for 30 seconds. Add the broth, lemongrass, lime peel, and chile, cook on high for 8 minutes, then strain. Return the broth to the casserole, add the shrimp and mushrooms, and cook on medium until the shrimp are just pink, about 2 minutes. Add the lime juice and fish sauce and serve as above.

Seafood and Poultry

Steamed Savory Custard
Kung Pao Scallops
Sweet and Sour Fish
  with Pineapple Fried Rice
Stuffed Steamed Trout
Swordfish with Miso-Mustard Sauce
Sesame Fish Cakes
Salmon Packets with Black Bean Sauce
My Uncle's Poached Fish
Fish with Sichuan Chili Sauce
Seafood and Asparagus Stir-Fry
Lobster with Sizzling Ginger-Chili Oil
Popping Clams with Sizzling Rice
Braised Dried Oysters with Black Moss
Clams in Black Bean Sauce
Steamed Tofu with Shrimp Mousse
Crab Foo Yung
Thai Barbecued Chicken
Lemon Chicken
Cantonese Roast Chicken
  with Honey-Hoisin Glaze
Double-Steamed Chicken with Herbs
Red-Cooked Chicken Drumettes
Chicken and Taro Casserole
Baked Stuffed Chicken Breasts
Fruited Sweet and Sour Chicken
Duck and Walnut Salad
Five-Spice Crispy Duck
Baked Smoke-Flavored Duck
Braised Eight-Precious Duck
Turkey and Vegetable Stir-Fry
Curried Turkey in a Noodle Nest
Roast Turkey, Chinese Style
Soy and Ginger Braised Turkey Breast

Seafood

As a boy growing up on the southern coast of China, I ate fish and shellfish daily. Later, while training in Hong Kong, I learned to cook many classic seafood dishes from masters. When you prepare fish or other seafood, remember the first, second, and third rules of seafood cookery: freshness, freshness, and freshness. It doesn't matter which method of preparation you choose, freshness is 90 percent of the formula. My favorite way to enjoy fresh seafood is simply to steam it with a few slices of ginger and green onion. Grilled, pan-fried, deep-fried—no matter how seafood is prepared, it's delicate and delicious.

Steamed Savory Custard

4 eggs, lightly beaten
1 green onion (including top), thinly sliced
1 teaspoon sesame oil
¼ teaspoon salt
⅛ teaspoon white pepper
1½ cups chicken broth
½ cup cooked, flaked crabmeat, small cooked shrimp, or diced cooked ham

Smooth and velvety, this cloudlike custard studded with crabmeat and green onion is good for brunch, lunch, or supper. It's a very popular dish in Japanese cuisine as well as Chinese homestyle cooking. With this steaming technique, you cook it in less than 20 minutes—one half the time it takes for oven baking.

Serves 4

1. Combine the eggs, green onion, sesame oil, salt, and pepper in a bowl. Stir in the broth until evenly blended, then stir in the crabmeat.

2. Place a steaming rack in a wok and add water to just below the level of the rack. Bring it to a boil and reduce the heat so the water simmers gently. Divide the egg mixture equally among four individual custard cups. Carefully set the cups on the rack, cover, and steam until a knife inserted in the center of the custard comes out clean, 18 to 20 minutes.

TIP: Keep the steaming water at a gentle simmer so the eggs will stay creamy. If you use frozen crabmeat or shrimp, pat it very dry between towels before combining it with the eggs. Any excess water will spoil the creamy texture of the custard.

Kung Pao Scallops

¾ pound sea scallops

Marinade
1 teaspoon sesame oil
2 teaspoons cornstarch
¼ teaspoon salt
Pinch of white pepper

Sauce
⅓ cup chicken broth
3 tablespoons
  balsamic vinegar or
  Chinese dark rice vinegar
2½ tablespoons soy sauce
5 teaspoons sugar
1½ teaspoons sesame oil

✿

1 small green or red
  bell pepper, seeded
1 small onion
2 stalks celery
1 can (15 ounces) whole
  bamboo shoots
3 tablespoons vegetable oil
2 teaspoons minced ginger
1 teaspoon minced garlic
6 whole dried chile peppers
½ teaspoon crushed
  red pepper
1½ teaspoons cornstarch
  dissolved in
  1 tablespoon water

You pronounce the "pao" in this recipe name like "pow," and that's the kind of flavor punch you get in this specialty from Sichuan. There's plenty of ginger, garlic, and fiery red peppers to dazzle the most jaded taste buds.

Serves 4

1. Cut the scallops in half horizontally. Combine them with the marinade ingredients in a medium bowl and stir to coat. Set aside for 30 minutes. Combine the sauce ingredients in another bowl.

2. Cut the bell pepper and onion into 1-inch squares. Cut the celery diagonally into ½-inch slices. Cut the bamboo shoots into 1-inch cubes. Place a wok or wide frying pan over high heat until hot. Add 2 tablespoons of the vegetable oil, swirling to coat the sides. Add the scallops and stir-fry until opaque, about 2 minutes. Remove the scallops to a bowl. Add the remaining 1 tablespoon of oil to the wok. Add the ginger, garlic, whole red peppers, and crushed red pepper. Slightly pressing the peppers into the oil with the back of a spatula, cook, stirring, until fragrant, about 10 seconds. Add the bell pepper, onion, celery, and bamboo shoots and stir-fry for 30 seconds. Tipping the bowl of scallops slightly, pour the accumulated juices into the wok and add the sauce. Cover and cook for 1 minute. Return the scallops to the wok. Add the cornstarch solution and cook, stirring, until the sauce boils and thickens.

VARIATION: You can cook just about any meat, poultry, or seafood *kung pao* style. The sauce can also be made ahead of time; simply omit the scallops and the diced vegetables from the above recipe. Keep the sauce on hand in a jar in the refrigerator, and when you're ready to use it, stir-fry your choice of meat and vegetables and stir in the sauce.

Sweet and Sour Fish with Pineapple Fried Rice

Batter
1 egg, lightly beaten
¼ cup cornstarch
¼ teaspoon salt
Pinch of white pepper

❀

4 tablespoons vegetable oil
1 pound red snapper fillets, cut into 1- by 2-inch pieces

Fried Rice
1 teaspoon minced ginger
1 teaspoon minced garlic
2 green onions (including tops), thinly sliced
1 red bell pepper, seeded and cut into ¼-inch squares
3 cups cooked long-grain rice
¼ cup chicken broth
2 tablespoons soy sauce
1 teaspoon sesame oil
¼ teaspoon white pepper

❀

1 can (8 ounces) pineapple tidbits, drained (reserve juice)
½ cup Sweet and Sour Sauce (Variation, page 70) or bottled sweet and sour sauce

Sweet and sour lovers, this one's for you. And it's as easy as 1-2-3: Batter and pan-fry the fish fillets; meanwhile, heat some sauce from the fridge; then stir up some fried rice in the same wok you used to cook the fish.

Serves 4

1. Combine the batter ingredients in a medium bowl; set aside.

2. Place a wide nonstick frying pan over medium-high heat until hot. Add 2 tablespoons of the vegetable oil, swirling to coat the surface. Dip the fish pieces into the batter, letting the excess drip off. Add half the fish to the pan and cook until lightly browned, about 2 minutes on each side. Lift out and drain on paper towels; keep warm. Add 1 tablespoon of oil to the pan and cook the remaining fish.

3. After all the fish is cooked, heat the remaining 1 tablespoon of oil in the same pan until hot. Add the ginger, garlic, and green onion and cook, stirring, until fragrant, about 10 seconds. Add the bell pepper and rice, separating the grains of rice with the back of a spoon. Reduce the heat to medium; cook and toss for 1 minute. Add the broth, soy sauce, sesame oil, and white pepper and cook, stirring, for 3 minutes. Toss with half of the pineapple pieces; keep warm. Meanwhile, bring the sweet and sour sauce and the remaining pineapple pieces to a boil in a small saucepan over medium-high heat. Pour the sauce over the fish and serve the fried rice on the side.

TIPS: If bottled sweet and sour sauce is too thick, add a small amount of pineapple juice.

Rock cod or other mild white fish fillets can be used in place of red snapper.

46

Stuffed Steamed Trout

2 trout (each about 12 ounces)

Marinade

1 tablespoon dry sherry or Chinese rice wine
½ teaspoon salt
¼ teaspoon white pepper

Sauce

3 tablespoons soy sauce
½ teaspoon sesame oil
1 teaspoon sugar

✿

2 green onions (including tops)
4 thin slices ginger, slivered
2 ounces ham, cut into matchstick pieces
Slivered green onion and ginger for garnish
2 tablespoons vegetable oil
Cilantro (Chinese parsley) sprigs for garnish

I always catch big trout, so each one is large enough for two people to share. If you catch (or buy) smaller fish, reduce the steaming time by a few minutes. The goal is to cook the fish just until it begins to flake so it will retain its mountain-lake freshness.

Serves 4

1. Score both sides of the fish with 3 diagonal cuts, ¾ inch deep. Combine the marinade ingredients on a deep plate large enough to hold the fish. Add the fish, turn to coat, and set aside for 30 minutes. Combine the sauce ingredients in a small bowl; set aside.

2. Cut one green onion into 2-inch pieces; crush slightly. Cut the remaining green onion into 2-inch slivers. Place the crushed green onion and half of the ginger and ham into the fish cavities. Tuck the slivered green onion and remaining ginger and ham into the diagonal cuts on the outside. Place the fish in a 9-inch heatproof glass pie pan.

3. Place a steaming rack in a wok, add water to just below the level of the rack, and bring to a boil. Place the pan of fish on the rack, cover, and steam until the center of the fish is opaque, about 15 minutes. Remove the pan, pour off and discard the juices. If desired, transfer the fish to a platter. Sprinkle the fish with slivered green onion and ginger. Heat the vegetable oil in a small saucepan until it just begins to smoke; pour it over the fish. Immediately pour the sauce over the fish. Garnish with cilantro sprigs.

MICROWAVE METHOD: In step 3, place the stuffed fish in a microwave-safe dish, cover, and cook on high until the flesh is just opaque, about 8 minutes. Let stand 2 minutes before serving.

Swordfish with Miso-Mustard Sauce

Sauce
¼ cup chicken broth
3 tablespoons white miso
2 tablespoons rice vinegar
2 tablespoons honey
1 tablespoon Japanese
   rice wine (sake)
2 teaspoons prepared
   Chinese-style mustard
Pinch of white pepper

❀

4 swordfish steaks,
   about ¾ inch thick
   (1½ to 2 pounds)
1 lemon, cut into 6 wedges

Made from soybeans and other grains, miso is packed with protein and is prized by Japanese cooks for its sweet-salty-savory flavor. With fish, I prefer white miso. It is less salty than the darker kinds and blends beautifully in this zippy mustard sauce. Chinese-style fermented soybean sauce is too dark and too salty for this dish.

Serves 4

Whisk the sauce ingredients together in a small bowl until evenly blended. Brush one side of the fish steaks with a little sauce and place them sauce side up on a rack in a foil-lined baking pan. Broil 3 to 4 inches from the heat for 4 minutes, turn, and brush with a little more sauce. Broil until the center of the fish is just opaque, 3 or 4 more minutes. Pour the remaining sauce onto a serving platter, place the fish on top of the sauce, and squeeze 2 of the lemon wedges over the fish. Garnish with the remaining lemon wedges.

TIP: Shredded daikon (white radish) makes a terrific garnish for this dish. Chill the daikon shreds in ice water for 30 minutes before serving so they become crisp and crystal white.

MICROWAVE METHOD: Place the fish in a shallow microwave-safe casserole, combine the sauce ingredients, and pour the sauce on top of the fish. Cover and cook on high until the center of the fish is just opaque, 7 to 8 minutes. Let stand 2 minutes. Serve and garnish as above.

Sesame Fish Cakes

Fish Cakes
¾ pound fresh red snapper
  or rock cod fillets
¼ cup finely chopped
  water chestnuts
2 tablespoons finely chopped
  red bell pepper
1 green onion (including
  top), minced
1 teaspoon chopped cilantro
  (Chinese parsley)
1 egg white
1 teaspoon cornstarch
¾ teaspoon salt
Pinch of white pepper

Coating
½ cup dried bread crumbs
2 tablespoons sesame seeds
♣
Vegetable oil for
  deep-frying
Red bell pepper slivers
  for garnish
Shredded seaweed (nori)
  for garnish

Being clever with your cleaver comes in handy when you make fish cakes. Of course, a food processor chops the fish even faster. Moist on the inside, crunchy and colorful on the outside, these savory little cakes make a colorful first course for any Asian or Western meal.

Makes 6 cakes

1. Chop the fish finely with a cleaver or in a food processor. Combine it with the remaining fish cake ingredients in a medium bowl and mix well. Shape the mixture into six 2-inch cakes. Combine the bread crumbs and sesame seeds in a shallow bowl. Dredge the fish cakes in the coating on both sides.

2. Set a wok in a ring stand and add oil to a depth of about 2 inches. Heat the oil to 360° and adjust the heat to medium-high. Slide the fish cakes into the oil and cook until golden brown, about 1½ minutes on each side. Remove the cakes with a skimmer and drain them on paper towels. Garnish with bell pepper slivers and shredded seaweed.

TIPS: You can use any fresh white fish to make this recipe. Some frozen fish tends to be dry and lacks the binding quality necessary for these cakes.

Nori is most familiar as the dried seaweed wrapper for rolled sushi. Look for it in Japanese stores.

VARIATION: If you prefer, you can pan-fry the fish cakes in 1 tablespoon of vegetable oil. Cook for 2½ minutes on each side or until golden.

Salmon Packets with Black Bean Sauce

4 dried black mushrooms

Topping

3 tablespoons preserved black beans, rinsed, drained and coarsely chopped
3 green onions (including tops), slivered
2 tablespoons shredded ginger
2 teaspoons minced garlic
1 teaspoon sugar

Marinade

2 tablespoons soy sauce
2 tablespoons dry sherry or Chinese rice wine
1 teaspoon sesame oil
1 teaspoon cornstarch
⅛ teaspoon white pepper

✿

1½ pounds salmon fillet, skinned and cut into 4 portions
1 tablespoon sesame oil
Lemon wedges for garnish

This is salmon at its best. An envelope of foil or parchment seals in both juices and flavor, keeping the salmon wonderfully moist. The zesty black bean topping enhances, but never obscures, the salmon's natural flavor.

Serves 4

1. Soak the mushrooms in warm water to cover for 30 minutes; drain. Cut off and discard the stems and thinly slice the caps. Combine the mushrooms with the topping ingredients in a bowl and set aside. Combine the marinade ingredients in a wide, shallow bowl. Add the salmon and turn it once to coat it. Cover and refrigerate for 30 minutes.

2. Preheat the oven to 400°. To make each packet, place a 12-inch square of aluminum foil on a flat work surface. Brush the center of the foil with a small amount of sesame oil and place a piece of salmon in the center. Spread a quarter of the topping over the fish. Fold the foil over to cover the fish; fold all edges to seal.

3. Place the packets in a shallow baking pan and bake 15 minutes or until the center of the fish is opaque. To test, cut a tiny slit through the foil into the fish. Serve with lemon wedges.

MICROWAVE METHOD: Follow the folding instructions in step 2, using parchment paper rather than foil and creasing the edges well to seal. Arrange the packets on a 9-inch microwave-safe glass pie pan and cook on medium-high until the salmon is flaky, 4 to 5 minutes.

My Uncle's Poached Fish

4 slices ginger, crushed
1 green onion (including top), lightly crushed
1 teaspoon salt
1½ pounds firm white fish fillets, such as cod, halibut, or sea bass, each cut ¾ inch thick

Sauce

1 tablespoon vegetable oil
1 teaspoon minced ginger
⅓ cup rice vinegar
3 tablespoons catsup
2 tablespoons soy sauce
3 tablespoons (packed) brown sugar
½ teaspoon hot pepper sauce or chili oil
2 teaspoons cornstarch dissolved in 4 teaspoons water

❀

1 green onion (including top), cut into 1½-inch slivers

When I was a young boy, my uncle and I would wake up before dawn hoping to catch some big fish in the local river. Most of the time our tiring efforts were unsuccessful; we often ended up telling stories about the fish that got away. If you are not a fisherman, visit your local fish market. Any white fish fillet will taste good in this dish.

Serves 4

1. Pour 2 inches of water into a wok or pan large enough to hold the fish. Add the ginger, crushed green onion, and salt and bring to a boil. Reduce the heat to low. Add the fish, cover, and simmer until the fish turns opaque, 6 to 8 minutes. Lift the fish out with a slotted spoon. Drain it briefly and keep it warm.

2. While the fish is cooking, prepare the sauce. Place a medium saucepan over high heat until hot. Add the oil, swirling to coat the surface. Add the ginger and cook, stirring, until fragrant, about 10 seconds. Add the rice vinegar, catsup, soy sauce, brown sugar, and hot pepper sauce and mix well. Add the cornstarch solution and cook, stirring, until the sauce boils and thickens. Pour the sauce over the fish and garnish with green onion slivers.

MICROWAVE METHOD: Fill a 3- to 4-quart microwave-safe casserole with 2 inches of water and heat on high until boiling, about 7 minutes. Add the ginger, crushed green onion, salt, and fish, cover, and cook on high for 4 minutes. Let stand until the fish is flaky, about 2 minutes. Combine the sauce ingredients in a 2-cup microwave-safe bowl and cook uncovered on high until hot, about 3 minutes. Lift the fish out of the poaching liquid and transfer it to a platter; top with the sauce and garnish with green onion slivers.

Fish with Sichuan Chili Sauce

Sauce

⅔ cup chicken broth
1 tablespoon dry sherry or
  Chinese rice wine
2 teaspoons soy sauce
2 teaspoons sesame oil
1½ teaspoons rice vinegar
1½ teaspoons
  Sichuan chili paste
1½ teaspoons cornstarch
½ teaspoon sugar
¼ teaspoon ground toasted
  Sichuan peppercorns
  (see page 17)

✿

1 pound rock cod fillets,
  about ¾ inch thick
⅔ cup cornstarch
½ teaspoon salt
¼ teaspoon black pepper
1 egg
3 tablespoons vegetable oil
1 tablespoon minced garlic
1 teaspoon minced ginger

Other than steaming Cantonese style, this is my favorite way of preparing fish. Lightly coated with a cornstarch batter and pan-fried in a wok, fish fillets or steaks come out crisp outside and meltingly tender inside, ready to receive the pungent sauce.

Serves 4

1. Combine the sauce ingredients in a small bowl; set aside. Cut the fish into serving-size pieces. Lightly score the fish on both sides with shallow diagonal cuts ½ inch apart. Score again at an angle to the first cuts, making a diamond pattern.

2. Combine the cornstarch, salt, and pepper in a shallow bowl. Lightly beat the egg in another shallow bowl. Dip each piece of fish in the egg, drain briefly, then dredge in the cornstarch mixture; shake off the excess.

3. Place a wok or wide frying pan over medium-high heat until hot. Add 2 tablespoons of the vegetable oil, swirling to coat the sides. Add the fish and cook for 3 minutes, turn, and add 2 more teaspoons of oil. Continue cooking until the fish is golden brown and the center is opaque, 3 to 4 more minutes. Transfer the fish to a platter, cover loosely, and keep warm.

4. Wipe the wok clean and turn the heat to high. Add the remaining teaspoon of oil, swirling to coat the sides. Add the garlic and ginger and cook, stirring, until fragrant, about 10 seconds. Stir in the sauce and cook, stirring, until it boils and thickens. Pour the sauce over the fish.

TIP: Don't coat the fish too much ahead of time. Doing it at the last minute ensures a crisp crust.

Seafood and Asparagus Stir-Fry

Marinade
1 tablespoon dry sherry or
   Chinese rice wine
1 teaspoon cornstarch
¼ teaspoon salt
Pinch of white pepper

❀

½ pound medium raw shrimp,
   shelled and deveined
¼ pound sea scallops,
   cut in half horizontally
½ pound asparagus
2 tablespoons vegetable oil
2 teaspoons minced garlic
½ cup canned baby corn,
   drained and cut in half
   diagonally
½ cup whole water chestnuts
½ cup chicken broth
2 tablespoons dry sherry or
   Chinese rice wine
1 teaspoon sesame oil
½ teaspoon sugar
½ teaspoon salt
Pinch of white pepper
2½ teaspoons cornstarch
   dissolved in
   5 teaspoons water

I get excited just thinking about fresh asparagus, which I never tasted until I came to North America. When asparagus is combined with shrimp, scallops, baby corn, and water chestnuts in this dish, it's almost too beautiful to eat.

Serves 4

1. Combine the marinade ingredients in a medium bowl. Add the shrimp and scallops; stir to coat. Set aside for 30 minutes. Snap off and discard the tough ends of the asparagus and cut the spears diagonally into 1½-inch pieces.

2. Place a wok or wide frying pan over high heat until hot. Add the vegetable oil, swirling to coat the sides. Add the garlic and cook, stirring, until fragrant, about 10 seconds. Add the shrimp and scallops; stir-fry for 2 minutes or until the scallops turn opaque and the shrimp turn pink. Remove the seafood from the wok. Add the asparagus, baby corn, water chestnuts, and broth; cover and cook for 2 minutes. Add the sherry, sesame oil, sugar, salt, and pepper; mix well. Return the seafood to the wok and add the cornstarch solution. Cook, stirring, until the sauce boils and thickens. Serve immediately.

VARIATION: You can use all shrimp if you prefer.

Lobster with Sizzling Ginger-Chili Oil

2 lobster tails
    (about 8 ounces each),
    thawed if frozen
3 thin slices ginger
2 green onions (including
    tops), cut in half
10 cilantro (Chinese
    parsley) sprigs

Sizzling Ginger-Chili Oil
¼ cup vegetable oil
1 green onion (including
    top), cut into 1½-inch
    slivers
1 tablespoon slivered ginger
½ teaspoon minced garlic
2 whole dried chile peppers
1 teaspoon sesame oil
¼ teaspoon salt
1 tablespoon soy sauce
❀
Cilantro (Chinese parsley)
    sprigs for garnish

An unusual method of cutting the lobster shell results in an especially attractive presentation. Quickly steamed over fragrant seasonings, the luscious meat curls tenderly over the shell. Then it's drizzled with a sizzling, spicy sauce—absolutely beautiful and delicious!

Serves 2

1. With scissors, cut lengthwise along the top of each lobster shell to the end of the tail, leaving the fan end intact. Spread the shell open and carefully pry out the meat, leaving it attached at the fan end; lay the meat over the top of the shell.

2. Crush the ginger, green onions, and cilantro sprigs with the flat side of a cleaver to bruise them slightly. Place them in a wok and add a steaming rack. Pour in water to just below the level of the rack; bring it to a boil.

3. Place the lobster, meat side up, in a heatproof dish and set the dish on the rack. Cover and steam until the lobster meat turns opaque, about 6 minutes. Transfer the lobster to a warm serving platter.

4. Heat the vegetable oil in a small saucepan until hot. Stir in the slivered green onion, ginger, garlic, chiles, sesame oil, and salt. Remove from the heat and stir in the soy sauce (the oil will sizzle). Immediately drizzle the oil over the lobster. Garnish with cilantro sprigs.

TIP: This dish can also make an attractive appetizer for four.

Popping Clams with Sizzling Rice

1 tablespoon vegetable oil
1 teaspoon minced garlic
2 serrano or jalapeño chile
  peppers, thinly sliced
2 green onions (including
  tops), thinly sliced
2 teaspoons chili paste
3 cups chicken broth
3 bottles (8 ounces each)
  clam juice
¼ cup chopped cilantro
  (Chinese parsley)
2 tablespoons fresh
  lime juice
2 teaspoons fish sauce
½ teaspoon sugar
16 to 20 small hard-shelled
  clams, scrubbed
¼ pound sea scallops,
  sliced horizontally in half
1 cup sliced mushrooms
1 package (about 1 pound)
  firm tofu, drained and
  cut into ½-inch cubes
Vegetable oil for deep-frying
8 two-inch square rice
  crusts (see Tip)
Cilantro (Chinese parsley)
  sprigs for garnish

Hot and spicy seasonings from Southeast Asia flavor this wonderful, very impressive soup. You won't hear the clams pop open—the sign that they are cooked—but get ready for plenty of sizzle when you slide the rice crusts into the fiery brew.

Serves 4 to 6

1. Place a wok or 6-quart pot over high heat until hot. Add the vegetable oil, swirling to coat the sides. Add the garlic, chiles, green onions, and chili paste and cook, stirring, until fragrant, about 10 seconds. Add the chicken broth, clam juice, chopped cilantro, lime juice, fish sauce, and sugar. Bring to a boil. Add the clams; cook until the clam shells open, about 5 minutes. Add the scallops, mushrooms, and tofu and cook until the scallops turn opaque, about 2 minutes. Keep warm while preparing the rice crusts.

2. Set a wok in a ring stand and add oil to a depth of about 2 inches. Place over high heat until the oil reaches 375°. Add the rice crusts, half at a time, and cook them, turning constantly, until puffed, about 15 seconds. Lift the crusts out and drain them on paper towels.

3. Pour the clams and broth into a warmed serving bowl and carry it to the table. Bring the hot fried rice crusts to the table and carefully slide them into the broth. Garnish with cilantro sprigs.

TIP: Look for rice crusts in Chinese markets.

Braised Dried Oysters with Black Moss

¼ pound dried oysters
½ ounce dried black moss
1 tablespoon vegetable oil
1 teaspoon minced ginger
1 tablespoon chopped shallot
1 green onion (including top), thinly sliced
1 cup chicken broth
1 tablespoon dry sherry or Chinese rice wine
1 teaspoon sesame oil
2 teaspoons cornstarch dissolved in 4 teaspoons water
8 to 12 iceberg lettuce cups, washed and chilled
Cilantro (Chinese parsley) sprigs for garnish (optional)

To the Chinese, dried oysters, *ho see* in Cantonese, symbolize good business; black moss, *fat choy* in Cantonese, offers prosperity; and lettuce, *sung choy,* prophesies wealth. Serve them together in this special New Year's dish, and good fortune is guaranteed to come your way.

Serves 6 to 8

1. Rinse the dried oysters and soak them in 1½ cups warm water for 1 hour. Drain, reserving 1 cup of the soaking liquid. Soak the black moss in warm water to cover for 30 minutes and drain.

2. Place a wok or wide frying pan over high heat until hot. Add the vegetable oil, swirling to coat the sides. Add the ginger, shallot, and green onion and cook, stirring, for 30 seconds. Add the oysters and stir-fry for 1 minute. Add the reserved oyster soaking liquid and the broth. Spread the moss in an even layer over the oysters. Reduce the heat to medium-low. Cover and simmer until the oysters are tender, about 30 minutes. Stir in the sherry and sesame oil. Add the cornstarch solution and cook, stirring, until the sauce boils and thickens.

3. Arrange the lettuce cups on a serving platter and spoon the oyster mixture into them. Garnish with cilantro sprigs, if desired.

TIPS: Whole leaves of iceberg lettuce are a popular wrapper for foods to be eaten without chopsticks. Use good-sized inner leaves that come off the head in one piece.

Black moss, also called hairlike seaweed or hair vegetable, is often steamed with simple seasonings or used in broths. It is available in Chinese markets and herbal stores.

Clams in Black Bean Sauce

1 tablespoon vegetable oil
1 tablespoon Chinese
  preserved black beans,
  rinsed, drained, and
  coarsely chopped
1 teaspoon minced garlic
1 serrano or jalapeño chile,
  thinly sliced
1 tablespoon dry sherry or
  Chinese rice wine
2 teaspoons soy sauce
½ teaspoon sugar
2 pounds small hard-shell
  clams, well scrubbed
⅓ cup chicken broth
1 teaspoon sesame oil
1½ teaspoons cornstarch
  dissolved in
  1 tablespoon water
1 green onion (including
  top), thinly sliced

This deliciously spicy dish is one of the most popular items served in Cantonese seafood restaurants. One taste will convince you to try it again—and again. You can buy the preserved black beans in Asian markets and in selected supermarkets across the country.

Serves 4 to 6

Place a wok or wide frying pan over high heat until hot. Add the vegetable oil, swirling to coat the sides. Add the black beans, garlic, and chile and cook, stirring, for 30 seconds. Stir in the sherry, soy sauce, and sugar. Add the clams, broth, and sesame oil; cover and cook until the clams open, about 6 minutes. Add the cornstarch solution and cook, stirring, until the sauce boils and thickens. Discard any clams that haven't opened by the time the sauce has thickened. Garnish with green onion.

Steamed Tofu with Shrimp Mousse

Shrimp Mousse

¼ pound medium raw
   shrimp, shelled and
   deveined
2 water chestnuts, coarsely
   chopped
½ teaspoon chopped cilantro
   (Chinese parsley)
1 egg white
1 tablespoon chicken broth
   or water
1½ teaspoons dry sherry or
   Chinese rice wine
1 teaspoon sesame oil
1 teaspoon cornstarch
¼ teaspoon salt

❀

1 package (about 1 pound)
   soft tofu, drained
1 tablespoon minced
   Smithfield ham
1 green onion (including
   top), chopped
2 teaspoons chopped cilantro
   (Chinese parsley)
1 tablespoon soy sauce
½ teaspoon sesame oil
Pinch of white pepper

I've taken a shortcut with this dish. Instead of painstakingly stuffing cubes of tofu with shrimp mousse, I completely cover each slice with mousse and steam the dish briefly. It's a snap to prepare, low in calories, packed with flavor, and it looks beautiful.

Serves 4

1. Coarsely chop the shrimp in a food processor. Add the remaining mousse ingredients and process until the shrimp are finely chopped, but not so long as to make a smooth paste. Cut the block of tofu in half horizontally; cut each piece in half lengthwise, then crosswise, to make 8 equal pieces.

2. Lay the tofu pieces side by side in a 9-inch pie pan or other heatproof dish. Spread shrimp mousse in an even layer over each piece. Sprinkle with ham, green onion, and cilantro.

3. Place a steaming rack in a wok, add water to just below the level of the rack, and bring to a boil. Place the dish on the rack, cover, and steam until the shrimp mousse turns pink, about 6 minutes. Remove the dish from the wok; carefully pour off the cooking juices. Sprinkle the tofu with soy sauce, sesame oil, and pepper.

TIP: Served Chinese style, this dish is placed in the center of the table and everyone helps himself. For individual servings, assemble the tofu and mousse in shallow ramekins that will fit in your steamer. The cooking time will not change.

Crab Foo Yung

Foo Yung Mixture

2 dried black mushrooms
2 eggs, lightly beaten
2 ounces (¼ cup) cooked
 crabmeat, flaked
1 green onion (including
 top), thinly sliced
½ teaspoon minced garlic
4 teaspoons dry sherry or
 Chinese rice wine
Pinch of white pepper

Sauce

¼ cup chicken broth
1 tablespoon oyster sauce
½ teaspoon cornstarch
✿
2 teaspoons vegetable oil

The Chinese symbol "foo yung" means extraordinary beauty — like the beauty of the peony. Traditional egg foo yung, a kind of Chinese omelet, is as fluffy and colorful as a flower in bloom. Although this version features crab, you can "foo yung" anything; like a flower, foo yung comes in different shapes and colors.

Serves 1

1. Soak the mushrooms in warm water to cover for 30 minutes; drain. Cut off and discard the stems and thinly slice the caps. Combine the mushrooms with the remaining foo yung ingredients in a medium bowl. Combine the sauce ingredients in a small saucepan; set aside.

2. Place a 6-inch nonstick frying pan over medium-high heat until hot. Add the oil, swirling to coat the bottom of the pan. Pour the foo yung mixture into the pan, tilting the pan so the egg mixture spreads evenly. Cook, without stirring, until the egg is set, then turn it to cook the other side. Meanwhile, bring the sauce to a boil over medium-high heat; cook, stirring, until it thickens. Slide the finished omelet onto a serving plate and pour the sauce over the top.

VARIATION: Substitute ¼ cup cooked baby shrimp, diced cooked ham, or water chestnuts for the crab.

Poultry

The Chinese call the chicken "king of the kitchen." I can think of no less than a thousand dishes which call for the chicken's presence. We eat it stir-fried, braised, steamed, fried, simmered, and of course, in soup. Like good grandmothers everywhere, mine believed a good bowl of chicken soup would cure whatever ailed me.

If chicken is king, then the main pretender to the throne is duck. Chinese cooks are famous for their repertoire of duck dishes, not only the famous roast ducks of Peking and Canton but also braised, steamed, and smoked versions. But I'll let you in on a secret: I wouldn't trade my mother's Eight-Precious Duck for any of them.

Turkey is unfamiliar in China, but I've been using it more and more these days. Ground turkey is a leaner substitute for ground pork in stuffings and meatballs, and the breast meat is fine for stir-frying.

Thai Barbecued Chicken

Marinade

3 tablespoons minced garlic
2 tablespoons finely chopped cilantro (Chinese parsley)
1 tablespoon sugar
1 teaspoon ground turmeric
1 teaspoon curry powder
½ teaspoon black pepper
3 tablespoons fish sauce

✿

8 chicken thighs (about 3 pounds)

This dish is similar to the mouth-watering chicken sold by street vendors in Bangkok, but you don't need to travel halfway around the world to enjoy its pungent flavor. Light the barbecue on a lazy summer weekend, or if time is short, bake the chicken in the oven.

Serves 4 to 8

1. Place the marinade ingredients in a food processor and process to a paste. Place the chicken in a sealable plastic bag with the marinade. Turn the bag several times so the chicken is well coated. Refrigerate for 4 hours or overnight, turning the bag occasionally to distribute the marinade.

2. Lift the chicken from the marinade and arrange it on a lightly greased grill 4 to 6 inches above a solid bed of low-glowing coals. Cook, turning frequently, until the meat near the bone is no longer pink when pierced, about 45 minutes. To cook indoors, place the chicken

pieces in a large shallow baking pan and bake uncovered at 375° until the meat is no longer pink near the bone, about 40 minutes.

TIP: If you bake the chicken, place it in a pan big enough so the pieces don't touch. This space allows the pan juices to evaporate and the chicken skin becomes crisp as it browns. Use two pans if necessary, reversing their positions in the oven halfway through cooking.

Lemon Chicken

Marinade
1 tablespoon soy sauce
1 tablespoon dry sherry or
    Chinese rice wine
1 teaspoon cornstarch
❀
2 chicken breast halves,
    skinned, boned, and cut
    into thin strips

Coating
1 cup finely chopped walnuts
½ cup cornstarch

Sauce
1 teaspoon grated lemon
    peel
1 teaspoon minced ginger
⅓ cup fresh lemon juice
⅓ cup chicken broth
2½ tablespoons sugar
2 teaspoons cornstarch
    dissolved in
    4 teaspoons water
❀
Vegetable oil for
    deep-frying

First you fry little nuggets of chicken breast coated with chopped walnuts. Then you top them with a light, refreshing, sweet-sour lemon sauce. No wonder this is such a popular dish in Chinese restaurants around the world.

Serves 4

1. Combine the marinade ingredients in a medium bowl. Add the chicken, stir to coat, and set aside for 30 minutes. Combine the coating ingredients in a shallow bowl; set aside. Combine the sauce ingredients in a small saucepan; set aside.

2. Set a wok in a ring stand; add oil to a depth of about 2 inches. Heat the oil to 360° and reduce the heat to medium-high. Remove the chicken strips from the marinade and roll them in the coating mixture. Fry them, half at a time, until golden brown, about 2 minutes. Lift them out with a slotted spoon and drain them on paper towels. Transfer them to a platter and keep them warm.

3. Give the sauce a stir and bring it to a boil over medium-high heat. Cook, stirring, until it thickens, then pour it over the chicken.

Cantonese Roast Chicken with Honey-Hoisin Glaze

1 whole frying chicken
  (about 3 pounds)
1 tablespoon soy sauce
½ teaspoon salt
½ teaspoon Chinese
  five-spice
2 thin slices ginger, crushed
2 cloves garlic, crushed

Glaze
1½ tablespoons soy sauce
1 tablespoon hoisin sauce
2 teaspoons honey
1 teaspoon sesame oil

The fantastic flavor and crispness of this dish result from rubbing the seasonings both under and over the skin, roasting the chicken uncovered, and brushing it with a honey-hoisin glaze during the last 10 minutes of roasting. It's great grilled too!

Serves 4 to 6

1. Rinse the chicken inside and out; pat it dry with paper towels. Starting at the neck opening, separate the skin and flesh with your fingers, being careful not to tear the skin. Work your fingers over each side of the breast and over the thigh areas.

2. In a small bowl, combine the soy sauce, salt, and five-spice. Rub half of the mixture over the chicken flesh, under the skin. Rub the remaining mixture on the outside of the chicken. Place the crushed ginger and garlic under the skin on the breast. Cover the chicken and refrigerate it for at least 2 hours or overnight. Just before cooking, combine the glaze ingredients in a small bowl; set aside.

3. Preheat the oven to 375°. Stand the chicken on a vertical roaster, or place it breast side up on a rack in a foil-lined shallow baking pan. Roast for 50 minutes, brush with the glaze, and continue to cook until the meat near the thigh bone is no longer pink when pierced, about 10 minutes.

VARIATION: To cook in a covered grill, prepare charcoal briquets in the usual manner. When the coals are beginning to turn grey, arrange them in a circle around the bottom of the grill. Set a shallow, disposable pan of water in the middle, place the chicken on a vertical roaster in the pan, and cover the grill. Open the top and bottom vents. Roast to an internal temperature of 165°, 30 to 40 minutes. Baste with the glaze during the last 10 minutes.

Double-Steamed Chicken with Herbs

1 package (4 ounces) dried
   mixed Chinese herbs
½ pound boneless
   chicken breasts or thighs,
   skin removed, cut into
   1-inch chunks
¼ pound boneless lean pork,
   cut into 1-inch chunks
6 dried black mushrooms
6 dried longans
½ ounce Smithfield ham,
   thinly sliced
4 cups water

This Chinese elixir of life is traditionally cooked in a Yunnan pot. Like an angel food cake pan or Mongolian hot pot, the Yunnan pot has a chimney coming up through the middle, which helps the heat (in this case from steam) circulate around the food more efficiently. You can also make the soup in a casserole set inside a larger steaming pot.

Some Chinese people consider this soup a tonic, and drink only the strained broth; but I see no reason not to eat the delicious meat as well.

Serves 6

1. Rinse the herbs well in warm water; drain. Place the chicken and pork in a medium pan and cover them with water. Bring to a boil and cook for 1 minute. Drain. Wash the mushrooms and cut off the stems. Place the herbs, chicken, pork, mushrooms, longans, and ham in a Yunnan pot, 7 inches in diameter, or a 2-quart casserole. Add the water and cover the pot.

2. Place a steaming rack in a wok. Pour in water to just below the level of the rack and bring it to a boil. Set the pot on the rack. Cover and steam for 3 hours, adding additional water as necessary. Strain the broth and serve hot.

NOTE: Packages of mixed dried herbs, which include various leaves, barks, and roots, are sold in Chinese herbal shops, and sometimes in larger Chinese groceries with herbal counters. Just ask for herbs for making chicken soup. Longans are a dried fruit related to lychees, also sold in well-stocked Chinese groceries.

Red-Cooked Chicken Drumettes

12 chicken drumettes OR
  6 chicken wings,
  cut in sections,
  wing tips discarded
1 tablespoon soy sauce

Sauce
1 cup chicken broth
3 tablespoons regular soy
  sauce
2 tablespoons dark soy sauce
2 tablespoons dry sherry or
  Chinese rice wine
1 tablespoon (packed)
  brown sugar
1 green onion (including
  top), cut into thirds
3 thin slices ginger, crushed
1 clove garlic, crushed
1 whole star anise
1 cinnamon stick
     ❀
2 teaspoons vegetable oil
2½ teaspoons cornstarch
  dissolved in
  2 tablespoons water

A red-cooked dish is my kind of lazy cooking. It is simple, delicious, and doesn't need constant attention. This recipe uses chicken drumettes, the larger, tender portion of the wing. A "drumette" is called that because of its resemblance to a chicken drumstick. By tradition, part of the sauce from a red-cooked dish is saved to cook other meats or poultry. The more you use a Master Sauce, the richer and rounder its flavors become.

Serves 4

1. Combine the chicken drumettes and soy sauce in a bowl; cover and refrigerate for 2 hours. Combine the sauce ingredients in a small bowl.

2. Place a medium pot over high heat until hot. Add the oil, swirling to coat the sides. Add the chicken and cook, stirring, until lightly browned, about 2 minutes. Add the sauce ingredients, stirring to mix evenly. Bring to a boil, reduce the heat, cover, and simmer until the chicken is tender when pierced, about 15 minutes. Remove ½ cup of sauce from the pot and place it in a small saucepan over medium-high heat. Bring it to a boil, add the cornstarch solution, and cook, stirring, until the sauce boils and thickens.

3. Lift the chicken from the pot with a slotted spoon and place it on a serving platter. Pour the thickened sauce over it. Cool the remaining sauce; cover and refrigerate it to use again.

TIP: Using two kinds of soy sauce is not a duplication in red-cooking. Regular soy sauce contributes a delicate flavor while dark soy gives a rich mahogany color. Try reusing this savory sauce with pork.

Chicken and Taro Casserole

Marinade

1 tablespoon soy sauce
1 tablespoon dry sherry or
   Chinese rice wine
1 teaspoon cornstarch

❖

1 pound boneless chicken
   thighs or breasts,
   skin removed,
   cut into 2-inch pieces
6 dried black mushrooms
1 pound taro

Sauce

2/3 cup chicken broth
3 tablespoons dry sherry or
   Chinese rice wine
2 tablespoons soy sauce
1/4 teaspoon black pepper

❖

2 tablespoons vegetable oil
5 large whole cloves garlic,
   peeled
1 large (2-inch) shallot,
   coarsely chopped
1 slice ginger
2 Chinese sausages (about
   2 ounces each), thinly
   sliced diagonally
2 green onions (including
   tops), cut into 1½-inch
   pieces

If you've been to Hawaii, you've probably seen the lush leaves of the taro plant. The leaves are as big as elephant ears. Depending on the variety, the tubers may vary from 4 ounces to several pounds and range in color from white to yellow to purple. Taro is one vegetable that is never eaten raw. When braised with poultry or meat, as in this casserole, it releases starch and thickens the flavorful juices.

Serves 6

1. Combine the marinade ingredients in a medium bowl. Add the chicken, turn to coat it, and set it aside for 30 minutes. Soak the mushrooms in warm water to cover for 30 minutes; drain. Cut off and discard the stems; slice the caps in half. Set aside. Peel the taro and cut it into bite-size chunks. Steam until tender when pierced, about 10 minutes, or microwave for 4 minutes. Combine the sauce ingredients in a small bowl.

2. Place a clay pot or other flameproof casserole over low heat; gradually increase the heat to medium-high. Add the oil, swirling to coat the surface. Add the garlic, shallot, and ginger and cook, stirring, until fragrant, about 10 seconds. Add the chicken and sausages and cook, stirring occasionally, until the chicken is lightly browned, about 2 minutes. Add the mushrooms, cooked taro, green onions, and sauce. Reduce the heat to medium-low, cover, and simmer, stirring occasionally, until the chicken is no longer pink when pierced, about 20 minutes.

TIPS: Frequently used clay pots do not need to be soaked, but if you use one only occasionally, soak it first in cold water to cover for 30 minutes. There is no need to dry it.

For a sweeter, even more mellow flavor, oven roast the garlic cloves and shallot until golden brown before cooking in the clay pot.

VARIATION: If you like curry, add 1 tablespoon of curry powder and 1/4 cup of coconut milk to the sauce before cooking.

Baked Stuffed Chicken Breasts

4 dried black mushrooms
4 large chicken breast halves,
  boned, skin on

Marinade
2 tablespoons soy sauce
2 tablespoons dry sherry or
  Chinese rice wine
1 teaspoon cornstarch
1 teaspoon sugar
½ teaspoon Chinese five-spice
Pinch of white pepper

Filling
4 cooked quail eggs,
  shells removed
½ small carrot, cut into
  2-inch matchstick pieces
½ small zucchini, cut into
  2-inch matchstick pieces
¼ cup sliced water chestnuts,
  cut into thin strips
1 green onion (including
  top), cut into 2-inch slivers
1 tablespoon minced ginger

✿

1 teaspoon sesame oil
Slivered green onion,
  for garnish

Which came first, the chicken or the egg? Don't waste time on the answer — just wrap boneless chicken breasts around quail eggs and strips of vegetables to make a good tasting, good looking individual entree. You can really impress your guests with this one.

Serves 4

1. Soak the mushrooms in warm water to cover for 30 minutes; drain. Cut off and discard the stems; slice the caps into matchstick pieces.

2. Remove the small muscle (fillet) from each chicken breast half; reserve them for other uses. Split each breast half horizontally almost all the way through, leaving one long edge attached, and open it up like a book. Lightly pound the breasts to an even thickness with the back edge of a cleaver blade or with a flat-surfaced mallet. Combine the marinade ingredients in a medium bowl. Add the chicken; stir to coat. Set aside for 30 minutes.

3. Preheat the oven to 350°. Drain the chicken breasts and discard the marinade. Place the flattened breasts, skin side down, on a work surface. Place a quail egg and a quarter of the remaining filling ingredients in the center of each breast. Roll up the breasts (do not fold in the sides). Place the rolls seam side down in a 9-inch baking pan and brush them with sesame oil.

4. Bake the rolls uncovered until the juices run clear when the chicken is pierced, 30 to 40 minutes. Transfer to a platter. Pour the pan juices over the rolls. Garnish with green onion.

Fruited Sweet and Sour Chicken

Marinade
1 tablespoon soy sauce
1 tablespoon dry sherry
2 teaspoons cornstarch
½ teaspoon sugar
1 egg, lightly beaten

✿

1 pound boneless, skinless
chicken thighs or breasts,
cut into 1-inch cubes
Cornstarch for dry-coating

Sauce
¼ cup fresh orange juice
¼ cup rice vinegar
3 tablespoons catsup
1 tablespoon soy sauce
3 tablespoons (packed)
brown sugar
½ teaspoon hot pepper
sauce or chili oil

✿

Oil for deep-frying
1 teaspoon minced ginger
1 small onion, cut into
1-inch cubes
1 bell pepper, seeded and
cut into 1-inch cubes
1 can (11 ounces) lychees,
drained
1 can (11 ounces) mandarin
oranges, drained
2 tablespoons lemon juice
1 tablespoon cornstarch
dissolved in
2 tablespoons water

Most of the early Chinese emigrants to the U.S. were from Canton; they brought their love of fresh ingredients and bright flavor combinations with them. Their sweet and sour dishes have become American favorites. Try this delicious version made with mandarin oranges and lychees.

Serves 6

1. Combine the marinade ingredients in a medium bowl. Add the chicken and stir to coat. Set aside for 30 minutes. Coat the chicken with cornstarch and shake off the excess. Combine the sauce ingredients in a small bowl; set aside.

2. Set a wok in a ring stand; add oil to a depth of about 2 inches. Place over high heat until the oil reaches 375°. Add the chicken a few pieces at a time and cook, turning occasionally, until golden brown, about 3 minutes. Lift out and drain on paper towels. Keep warm while cooking the remaining chicken.

3. Place a skillet or medium saucepan over high heat until hot. Add 1 tablespoon vegetable oil, swirling to coat the surface. Add the ginger and cook, stirring, until fragrant, about 10 seconds. Add the onion and cook for 1 minute or until softened. Add the bell pepper and cook for 1 minute. Add the lychees and sauce and mix well. Add the mandarin oranges, lemon juice, and chicken and toss to coat evenly. Add the cornstarch solution and cook, stirring, until the sauce thickens.

VARIATION: To prepare the Sweet and Sour Sauce separately, combine the sauce ingredients as above. Heat 1 tablespoon vegetable oil in a wok or skillet, add 1 teaspoon minced ginger, and cook until fragrant; add the sauce mixture and cook, stirring, until the sugar dissolves. Dissolve 1 tablespoon cornstarch in 2 tablespoons water, stir into the sauce and cook, stirring, until the sauce boils and thickens. Refrigerate until ready to use. Try it tossed in with stir-fried meats and vegetables, or reheated over fried fish or chicken.

70

Duck
and
Walnut Salad

½ cup walnut halves
½ of a Chinese roast duck

Dressing
½ cup vegetable oil
¼ cup rice vinegar
1 teaspoon Chinese prepared
 mustard
1 teaspoon honey

❁

½ cup matchstick pieces jicama
½ cup matchstick pieces celery
3 cups mixed salad greens

Next time you see crisp, shiny Cantonese roast ducks hanging in the window of a Chinese deli, pick up half a duck and turn it into this easy Western-style salad. Although Cantonese roast duck is sometimes confused with its Northern cousin Peking duck, it is much more highly seasoned and can be served hot or cold without a sauce. The more delicate Peking version is always served hot, with hoisin sauce and Mandarin pancakes or steamed buns.

Serves 2 as a main dish, 4 as a side dish

1. Preheat the oven to 350°. Bring about 2 cups of water to a boil in a medium saucepan. Add the walnuts and cook for 1 minute. Drain the nuts, pat them dry, spread them on a cookie sheet, and toast them in the oven until crisp and brown, 10 to 12 minutes. Let stand until cool.

2. Cut the duck breast from the carcass in one piece, with the skin attached. Cut it crosswise into very thin slices. Remove the remaining meat from the carcass and cut it into shreds.

3. Place ¼ cup of the toasted walnuts in a food processor or blender with the dressing ingredients. Process until well blended.

4. Set aside a few strips of jicama and celery for garnish. Place the rest, the salad greens, and the shredded duck meat in a large bowl. Add half the dressing, toss to mix well, and transfer to a serving platter. Arrange the duck breast slices on top. Garnish with the remaining walnuts and reserved jicama and celery strips. Serve the remaining dressing on the side.

Five-Spice Crispy Duck

1 duckling (4 to 5 pounds),
cleaned and trimmed
(see Tip)

Marinade
2 tablespoons grated
orange peel
2 teaspoons minced ginger
1 teaspoon minced garlic
4 whole star anise
¼ cup soy sauce
4 teaspoons sugar
2 teaspoons salt
1 teaspoon Chinese five-spice

Everyone loves the crackling skin and succulent meat of roast duck, but not everyone loves the layer of fat in the middle. With this technique, you steam the duck first so it sheds much of its fat, then roast it to brown and crisp the skin.

Serves 6

1. Place a steaming rack in a wok. Pour in water to just below the level of the rack and bring it to a boil. Place the duck breast side up on a heatproof dish and set the dish on the rack. Cover and steam for 30 minutes. Let cool slightly.

2. Preheat the oven to 375°. Combine the marinade ingredients and rub the marinade over the skin of the duck. Place the duck breast side down on a rack in a foil-lined roasting pan. Roast uncovered for 30 minutes. Protecting your hands with several layers of paper towel, turn the duck breast side up. Reduce the heat to 325° and roast until the skin is browned and crisp and the meat near the thigh bone is no longer pink when pierced, about 1 hour.

TIPS: To prepare a whole duck for cooking Chinese style, cut off and discard the excess neck skin and the tail and remove all the loose fat from around the cavity. With the tip of a small, sharp knife, lightly prick the skin around the legs and other fatty areas (you can see the pockets of fat under the skin). Take care not to pierce the meat under the fat layer.

Star anise, brown, eight-pointed, star-shaped seed pods with a strong licorice flavor, are often used in barbecues, stews, and braised dishes. Rather than one whole star anise, an equivalent of broken points will do. Sometimes it is hard to find a plastic bag of whole ones.

Baked Smoke-Flavored Duck

Marinade

1 green onion (including top), fincly chopped
2 teaspoons chopped ginger
2 tablespoons soy sauce
1 tablespoon hoisin sauce
1 tablespoon dry sherry or Chinese rice wine
¼ teaspoon Chinese five-spice
¼ teaspoon white pepper

✿

1 duckling (4 to 5 pounds), cleaned and trimmed (See Tip, page 72)
1 whole star anise
1 green onion (including top), crushed

Tea Mixture

⅔ cup black tea leaves
½ cup raw rice
¼ cup (packed) dark brown sugar
2 teaspoons Chinese five-spice

Glaze

3 tablespoons honey
1 tablespoon soy sauce
1 teaspoon sesame oil

To give duck a light and very delicate smoky flavor, Chinese cooks don't use mesquite or charcoal. They make smoke from a mixture of tea leaves, raw rice, brown sugar, and spices and let it swirl around the bird. It's all done neatly under a foil tent in the oven.

Serves 6 to 8

1. Combine the marinade ingredients in a large bowl. Add the duck and rub it inside and out with the marinade. Place the star anise and crushed green onion in the cavity. Cover and refrigerate overnight.

2. Place a steaming rack in a wok, pour in water to just below the level of the rack and bring it to a boil. Place the duck breast side up on the rack. Cover and steam for 45 minutes, adding additional water if necessary. Remove the duck from the steamer and pat it dry.

3. While the duck is steaming, prepare the pan for smoking as follows: Line the bottom of a deep roasting pan with heavy-duty foil. Combine the tea mixture ingredients on the foil, mix well, and spread in an even layer. Place an empty 2-inch-high can (such as a water chestnut can) at each end of the pan and position a wire rack large enough to hold the duck on the cans.

4. Preheat the oven to 400°. Place the duck on the rack. Cover the entire pan with a large sheet of foil, making a tent; seal the edges. Bake for 45 minutes. Meanwhile, combine the glaze ingredients in a small bowl. Remove the duck from the oven, remove the top sheet of foil, and brush the duck with glaze. Reduce the heat to 350°, return the duck to the oven, and bake uncovered until golden brown, 8 to 10 minutes.

5. Cut the duck into serving-size pieces and arrange them on a serving platter in the shape of a whole duck.

TIP: Served cold, this is a wonderful addition to an appetizer plate.

Braised Eight-Precious Duck

Marinade

1 tablespoon minced garlic
3 tablespoons soy sauce
1 tablespoon sugar
½ teaspoon salt

❀

1 duckling (4 to 5 pounds),
  cleaned and trimmed (see
  Tip, page 72)
12 dried black mushrooms

Broth Mixture

1 can (14½ ounces)
  chicken broth plus
  1 can of water
¼ cup red bean paste
2 teaspoons sugar
1 whole star anise

❀

2 tablespoons vegetable oil
6 cloves garlic, pressed
6 thin slices ginger
2 shallots, cut into wedges
1 leek (white part only),
  split lengthwise and cut
  into 2-inch strips
2 green onions, cut into
  2-inch pieces
1 can (8 ounces) bamboo
  shoots, drained and cut
  into 1½-inch pieces
1 can (8 ounces) whole
  water chestnuts, drained
1 pound taro or thin-
  skinned potatoes, peeled,
  cut into 1½-inch chunks
1 tablespoon cornstarch

This is a wonderful entree for a special meal, Chinese or Western, and a delightful change from roast duck. Slow braising makes an especially flavorful sauce, and leaves the meat so tender you can pull it from the bones with chopsticks.

Serves 6 to 8

1. Combine the marinade ingredients in a large bowl. Add the duck and set aside for 1 hour, turning occasionally. Soak the mushrooms in warm water to cover for 30 minutes; drain. Cut off and discard the stems; thinly slice the caps. Set aside.

2. Combine the broth mixture ingredients in a small bowl; set aside. Remove the duck from the marinade and pat it dry. Place a wok or wide frying pan over medium heat until hot. Add 1 tablespoon of the oil, swirling to coat the sides. Brown the duck well on all sides, transfer it to a plate, and set it aside.

3. Place a large pot over medium-high heat until hot. Add the remaining tablespoon of oil, swirling to coat the sides. Add the garlic, ginger, and shallots; cook, stirring, until fragrant, about 10 seconds. Stir in the leek, green onions, mushrooms, bamboo shoots, water chestnuts, and broth mixture. Add the duck, breast side down. Bring to a boil, reduce the heat to medium-low, cover, and cook for 1¼ hours, turning the duck over halfway through the cooking period. Add the taro or potato and cook for 30 to 35 minutes or until the duck is tender.

4. Remove the duck and vegetables to a serving platter. Dissolve the cornstarch in 2 tablespoons of water. Add the cornstarch solution to the liquid in the pot; cook, stirring, until the sauce boils and thickens. Serve half the sauce over the duck, and the rest over rice or noodles.

Turkey and Vegetable Stir-Fry

Marinade

1 tablespoon dry sherry or
   Chinese rice wine
1 teaspoon soy sauce
1 teaspoon cornstarch

❀

¼ pound ground turkey
1 tablespoon vegetable oil
1 teaspoon minced ginger
½ teaspoon minced garlic
¼ cup frozen peas and
   carrots, thawed
¼ cup coarsely chopped
   water chestnuts
1 green onion (including
   top), thinly sliced
¼ cup chicken broth
1 teaspoon soy sauce
½ teaspoon sesame oil
½ teaspoon cornstarch
   dissolved in
   1 teaspoon water
¼ cup chopped toasted
   walnuts
1 teaspoon chopped cilantro
   (Chinese parsley)

I never knew about turkey (or frozen peas and carrots, for that matter) when I was growing up in Guangzhou, China. It's a treat combining them in this easy, quick stir-fry. Serve it over rice or noodles.

Serves 1

1. Combine the marinade ingredients in a small bowl. Add the turkey, stirring to break it up and coat it with marinade. Cover and refrigerate for 30 minutes.

2. Place a wok or wide frying pan over high heat. Add the vegetable oil, swirling to coat the sides. Add the ginger and garlic and cook, stirring, until fragrant, about 10 seconds. Add the turkey and stir-fry, using the back of a spatula to break up the meat, until brown and crumbly, about 1½ minutes. Add the vegetables, broth, soy sauce, and sesame oil, cook for 1 minute, and add the cornstarch solution. Cook, stirring, until the sauce boils and thickens. Sprinkle with walnuts and cilantro just before serving.

TIPS: You can substitute lean ground beef for the turkey.

To toast the nuts, spread them in a shallow baking pan; bake uncovered in a preheated 350° oven, stirring occasionally, until toasty brown, 10 to 12 minutes.

Curried Turkey in a Noodle Nest

Marinade
1 tablespoon soy sauce
1 tablespoon dry sherry
½ teaspoon sugar

❀

½ pound boneless turkey
  breast, in thin slices

Sauce
¼ cup chicken broth
1 tablespoon soy sauce
1 teaspoon chili paste
2 teaspoons curry powder
2 teaspoons cornstarch
¼ teaspoon five-spice

Noodle Basket
½ pound fresh egg noodles
2 tablespoons beaten egg
1½ tablespoons oil
1 tablespoon cornstarch
Pinch of salt

❀

Vegetable cooking spray
2 tablespoons vegetable oil
1 teaspoon minced ginger
2 stalks celery, thinly sliced
1 small red bell pepper,
  seeded and cut diagonally
  into ½-inch pieces
2 ounces sugar snap peas or
  Chinese pea pods, ends
  and strings removed
2 green onions (including
  tops), cut diagonally
  into 1½-inch pieces
¼ cup chicken broth

Here's a garnish that's not just for show. After you savor the curried turkey, break the lacy noodle nest apart and nibble on the pieces.

Serves 4

1. Combine the marinade ingredients in a small bowl. Add the turkey and stir to coat. Set aside for 30 minutes. Combine the sauce ingredients in a small bowl.

2. Preheat the oven to 375°. Cook the noodles according to package instructions. Drain, rinse lightly, and drain again. Place the remaining noodle basket ingredients in a large bowl and mix well. Add the noodles and toss until evenly coated. Line a cookie sheet with parchment paper. Spray the outside of a flat-bottomed strainer basket or sieve (6 to 7 inches in diameter and 3 inches deep) with vegetable cooking spray. Place the strainer, open side down, on the lined cookie sheet. Arrange the noodles in a lace-like pattern over the bottom and around the sides of the strainer. Bake until golden brown and crispy, 15 to 20 minutes. Let stand until cool, then gently remove and place on a serving plate.

3. Place a wok or wide frying pan over high heat until hot. Add the vegetable oil, swirling to coat the sides. Add the ginger, and cook, stirring, until fragrant, about 10 seconds. Add the turkey, and stir-fry until no longer pink, about 2 minutes. Remove the turkey from the wok. Add the celery, bell pepper, peas, green onions, and broth, and stir to mix well. Cover and cook for 1 minute or until the vegetables are crisp-tender. Return the turkey to the pan. Stir the sauce to recombine, add it to the pan, and cook, stirring, until the sauce boils and thickens. Spoon the turkey mixture into the nest.

TIP: The traditional noodle nest is deep-fried. Because this baked version is more fragile, it is important to make it only from Chinese-style fresh egg noodles. Dried noodles and brands labeled "ready cooked" are not sticky enough to hold the nest together.

Roast Turkey, Chinese Style

1 turkey, 13 to 15 pounds

Marinade
3 tablespoons soy sauce
1 teaspoon Chinese five-spice
1 teaspoon black pepper
1 teaspoon minced garlic

Stuffing
8 dried black mushrooms
¼ cup dried shrimp
1 tablespoon vegetable oil
2 Chinese sausages
  (about 2 ounces each),
  thinly sliced
1 teaspoon minced garlic
3 green onions (including
  tops), thinly sliced
1 can (8 ounces)
  water chestnuts, coarsely
  chopped
2 tablespoons chopped
  cilantro (Chinese parsley)
3 tablespoons oyster sauce
1 tablespoon soy sauce
½ teaspoon white pepper
3 cups cooked glutinous or
  medium-grain rice

After sampling this tasty, crisp-skinned turkey with its special rice stuffing you may never go back to plain roast turkey. This bird's superb! Glutinous rice, a popular Chinese poultry stuffing, is often marketed as "sweet rice," and sometimes as "sticky rice."

Serves 8

1. Remove the giblets from the turkey; reserve them for other uses. Rinse the turkey inside and out and pat it dry with paper towels. Combine the marinade ingredients in a small bowl and rub them over the skin of the turkey. Cover and refrigerate for 2 hours or as long as overnight.

2. Soak the mushrooms and dried shrimp separately in warm water to cover for 30 minutes; drain. Cut off and discard the mushroom stems and thinly slice the caps. Leave the shrimp whole.

3. Place a wok or wide frying pan over high heat until hot. Add the oil, swirling to coat the sides. Add the sausage, shrimp, and garlic and stir-fry until the sausage is slightly crisp, about 2 minutes. Add the mushrooms, green onions, water chestnuts, and cilantro; cook for 1 minute. Stir in the oyster sauce, soy sauce, and pepper. Add the rice, mix well, and remove from the heat.

4. Preheat the oven to 350°. Spoon the stuffing into the turkey cavity; close it with trussing needles or sew it closed. Place the turkey on a rack in a foil-lined baking pan. Bake until the juices run clear when a thigh is pierced, about 3 hours. (Or, insert a meat thermometer in the center of one of the inside thigh muscles, being careful that the tip does not touch bone. Bake until the thermometer registers 180° to 185°.) During the last half of the roasting time, baste the turkey occasionally with pan juices.

TIP: If you make the stuffing ahead, let it cool, cover it, and refrigerate it until needed. If you use the stuffing while it is still warm, roast the turkey immediately after stuffing.

Soy and Ginger Braised Turkey Breast

1 whole turkey breast
  (about 4½ pounds)
  bone in, skin on
2 cups low-sodium soy sauce
2 cups water
½ cup dry sherry or
  Chinese rice wine
1 tablespoon ginger,
  coarsely chopped
1 whole star anise
  OR ¼ teaspoon anise seed
1 medium green onion,
  coarsely chopped
3 tablespoons (packed) light
  brown sugar
3 tablespoons sesame oil
  or vegetable oil
Lettuce leaves for garnish

Manhattan caterer Rick Rodgers showed me this variation on the classic "red-cooked" whole chicken. A whole turkey breast is about the same size, but contains a higher proportion of meat, and its smooth skin takes on the same deep mahogany color from slow cooking in a soy sauce mixture. This is an adaptation of the recipe that appears in his book *The Turkey Cookbook* (HarperCollins, 1990). It's delicious served hot, but it's even better at room temperature.

Serves 4 to 6

1. Rinse the turkey breast and pat it dry with paper towels. Combine the soy sauce, water, sherry, ginger, star anise, and green onion in a large saucepan; bring to a simmer over medium heat. Add the turkey breast, skin side up. Using a baster or large spoon, continuously baste the turkey breast with the braising liquid until it returns to a simmer, about 1 minute. Cover the pan tightly, and simmer on low heat for 20 minutes, basting twice. Turn the turkey breast over carefully with two wooden spoons; stir in the brown sugar. Cover and simmer 20 minutes longer, basting the turkey twice.

2. Remove the pan from the heat but keep it tightly covered. Let the turkey stand in the liquid for 1 hour, basting every 15 minutes. Turn the turkey breast over carefully with two wooden spoons and let it stand, covered, 1 hour longer, again basting every 15 minutes.

3. Remove the turkey breast from the braising liquid and place it on a washed surface. Brush the skin with sesame oil. For the best-looking presentation, chop the breast into pieces Chinese-style. With a heavy cleaver, chop the rib and backbone section away from the meat portion of the breast. Chop the breast in half vertically down the breastbone. Chop each breast portion crosswise into 3 or 4 pieces. Chop each piece in half vertically. (If you prefer, carve the turkey breast in the usual way.) To serve, line a serving platter with lettuce leaves and arrange the turkey pieces on top. Serve at room temperature with braising liquid as a dipping sauce.

Pork,
Beef,
and
Lamb

Pork

We Chinese are not big meat eaters, at least by Western standards. Meat is used more as a flavoring than as a main ingredient, and is always accompanied by vegetables. The most popular meat of all in Chinese cooking is pork; in fact, the Chinese words for "meat" and "pork" are the same.

One reason pork is so widely used is the way its flavor blends harmoniously with all kinds of wonderful ingredients. My Mom showed me how to prepare hundreds of delicious pork dishes when I was growing up.

Pork raised in this country today is leaner than ever before, and what fat remains is easily separated rather than marbled into the meat. All in all, it's a great source of protein, B vitamins, and flavor, making it an ideal meat for the modern diet.

Plum-Flavored Ribs

2 pounds pork spareribs
1 cup canned purple
  plums, pitted
¼ cup syrup from plum can
1 small clove garlic,
  crushed
1½ teaspoons dry sherry or
  Chinese rice wine
1½ teaspoons rice vinegar
1 tablespoon soy sauce
1 tablespoon honey
¼ teaspoon salt
¼ teaspoon crushed red
  pepper
1 tablespoon chicken broth
  or water (optional)

One bite, and you'll understand just how good "plum good" can be. And these spicy-sweet ribs are so easy. Just blend the marinade in the food processor, marinate the ribs for as long as convenient (4 hours to overnight), and bake.

Serves 4

1. Trim and discard excess fat from the ribs; lightly score the meaty side at 1-inch intervals. Place the ribs in a shallow pan. Combine the plums, syrup, garlic, sherry, vinegar, soy sauce, honey, salt, and red pepper in a food processor. Process to a smooth paste. Pour the mixture over the ribs, turning the meat to coat both sides. Cover and refrigerate 4 to 6 hours or overnight.

2. Preheat the oven to 450°. Remove the ribs from the marinade, drain them well, and place them on a rack in a foil-lined baking pan. Transfer the marinade to a small saucepan. Bake the ribs uncovered for 30 minutes. Reduce the heat to 350°, turn the ribs over, and bake for 10 minutes. Brush with marinade and continue

baking until the meat is tender when pierced with a knife, about 10 more minutes. Cut the ribs between the bones before serving. If you want to serve the ribs with a sauce, add the chicken broth to the remaining marinade and simmer over medium heat for 3 to 5 minutes. Pass the sauce at the table to spoon over the ribs.

Jing Do Pork Chops

1½ pounds pork chops, each about ¾ inch thick

Marinade

3 tablespoons dry sherry or Chinese rice wine
2 tablespoons soy sauce
2 teaspoons cornstarch

Sauce

¼ cup catsup
2 tablespoons rice vinegar
1 tablespoon soy sauce
1 tablespoon Worcestershire sauce
½ teaspoon hot pepper sauce
1 tablespoon sugar

❀

1 egg, lightly beaten
2 teaspoons cornstarch
¼ cup vegetable oil
1 teaspoon minced ginger
1 teaspoon minced garlic
1 tablespoon chopped cilantro (Chinese parsley)

This recipe is a cousin to the ever-popular Sweet and Sour Pork. *Jing do* means capital city, and usually refers to Beijing, the home of this dish.

Serves 6

1. Bone the pork chops and cut the meat into roughly 2-inch squares. With the flat side of a cleaver or a mallet, lightly pound the squares to ¼ inch thick. Combine the marinade ingredients in a large bowl. Add the pork and stir to coat. Cover and refrigerate for 2 hours. Combine the sauce ingredients in a small bowl and set aside.

2. Just before cooking, add the egg and cornstarch to the pork; mix well. Place a wok or wide frying pan over medium-high heat until hot. Add 2 tablespoons of the oil, swirling to coat the sides. Place half the meat in the wok; cook until it is no longer pink when slashed, about 2 minutes on each side. Remove. Cook the remaining meat with the remaining 2 tablespoons of oil; remove. Discard the pan drippings. Add the ginger and garlic to the wok and cook, stirring, until fragrant, about 10 seconds. Return the pork to the wok and add the sauce. Cook, stirring, for 30 seconds, coating the meat well with the sauce. Sprinkle with cilantro before serving.

Pork and Summer Squash Stir-Fry

Marinade

1 tablespoon soy sauce
2 teaspoons dry sherry or Chinese rice wine
1 teaspoon cornstarch
✿
¾ pound boneless lean pork, thinly sliced

Sauce

⅓ cup chicken broth
2 tablespoons soy sauce
½ teaspoon sesame oil
✿
1 medium zucchini
1 large yellow crookneck squash
2 tablespoons vegetable oil
2 teaspoons minced garlic
2 green onions (including tops), thinly sliced
1½ teaspoons cornstarch dissolved in
1 tablespoon water
½ cup coarsely chopped toasted walnuts

Did you ever grow zucchini? It seems like one day the plants are in bloom, and the next morning you discover a giant squash. You can give part of your harvest away to neighbors or, for fun, make this stir-fry and ask some neighbors over for dinner.

Serves 4

1. Combine the marinade ingredients in a small bowl. Add the pork, stir to coat, and set aside for 30 minutes. Combine the sauce ingredients in a small bowl. Cut the zucchini and crookneck squash into matchstick pieces.

2. Place a wok or wide frying pan over high heat until hot. Add the vegetable oil, swirling to coat the sides. Add the garlic and cook, stirring, until fragrant, about 10 seconds. Add the pork and stir-fry until it is no longer pink, about 2 minutes. Remove the pork to a serving dish. Add the zucchini, crookneck squash, and sauce to the wok, cover, and cook for 2 minutes. Return the pork to the wok, stir in the green onions, and add the cornstarch solution. Cook, stirring, until the sauce boils and thickens. Stir in the walnuts just before serving.

TIP: The more varieties of summer squash you use, the more colorful this dish will be. Try golden zucchini, the thicker, pale green English zucchini, or pattypan squash too.

Minced Pork with Preserved Fish

2 ounces Chinese preserved fish (see Tip)

Patty Mixture
¾ pound boneless pork butt
1 Chinese sausage (about 2 ounces), finely chopped
¼ cup chopped water chestnuts
1 egg white
¼ cup chicken broth
1 tablespoon dry sherry or Chinese rice wine
2 teaspoons sesame oil
1 teaspoon soy sauce
Pinch of white pepper
2 tablespoons cornstarch
❀
1 teaspoon finely shredded ginger
2 green onions (including tops), thinly sliced

Some kids have warm memories of their mom's kitchen smelling of sugar and spice. The wafting aroma that drew me to my Mom's kitchen in double-quick time was fermented fish steaming on a plump pork patty. It smelled up the whole house, but when it was done, wow— it tasted good.

Serves 4 to 6

1. Soak the preserved fish in water to cover for 15 minutes; drain. Cut the fish into thin slices and remove any bones.

2. In a food processor or with a cleaver, coarsely chop the pork. Place it in a large bowl with the remaining patty mixture ingredients and mix well. Spread the mixture evenly in a 9-inch glass pie pan. Top with the preserved fish, ginger, and 2 teaspoons of the green onion.

3. Place a steaming rack in a wok. Pour in water to just below the level of the rack and bring to a boil. Set the pie pan on the rack. Cover and steam over high heat until the pork is no longer pink (cut a slit to test), about 12 minutes. Sprinkle with remaining green onions before serving.

TIP: The preserved fish I use comes from Hong Kong or Macao as whole fish about 6 to 10 inches long, in plastic wrappers. Some packages are labeled "salted fish." It has fermented slightly in the drying process, giving it a different flavor than Western-style salt cod or other salted fish. You may also find it packed in oil in jars, the only real substitute.

Spiced Orange Pork Chops with Onions

Sauce
⅓ cup fresh orange juice
2 teaspoons grated orange peel
¼ cup chicken broth
1 tablespoon soy sauce
1 tablespoon (packed) brown sugar

✿

1 teaspoon salt
¼ teaspoon Chinese five-spice
4 pork chops, each about ½ inch thick (1 to 1½ pounds total)
1 tablespoon vegetable oil
1½ teaspoons minced garlic
1 teaspoon minced ginger
¼ teaspoon crushed red pepper
1 small onion, thinly sliced
2 teaspoons cornstarch dissolved in 4 teaspoons water
Orange slices for garnish
Orange peel, cut into thin strips for garnish

Braising is one of the most popular cooking techniques in many parts of China. You'll understand why once you sample these pork chops prepared in a tangy orange sauce.

Serves 4

1. Combine the sauce ingredients in a small bowl; set aside. Combine the salt and five-spice in a small bowl; sprinkle over the pork chops.

2. Place a wide nonstick frying pan over high heat until hot. Add 2 teaspoons of the oil, swirling to coat the bottom of the pan. Add the pork chops and brown for 2 minutes on each side; remove. Add the remaining teaspoon of oil to the pan, swirling to coat the surface. Add the garlic, ginger, red pepper, and onion and stir-fry until the onion is softened, about 2 minutes.

3. Return the pork chops to the pan; reduce the heat to low. Pour the sauce over the chops, cover, and simmer until the meat is no longer pink, 5 to 7 minutes. Transfer the chops to a warm serving platter. Add the cornstarch solution to the pan and cook, stirring, until the sauce boils and thickens. Pour over the chops. Garnish with orange slices and orange peel.

MICROWAVE METHOD: In step 2, combine the oil, garlic, ginger, red pepper, and onion in a shallow microwave-safe casserole and heat on high for 2 minutes. Stir, place the pork chops on top, and pour the sauce over the meat. Cover and cook on high until the pork is no longer pink, about 7 minutes. Remove the chops to a warm serving platter. Stir the cornstarch solution into the casserole, cover, and cook on high until the sauce boils and thickens, about 2 minutes. Serve as above.

Country-Style Sausage Patties

1 pound lean ground pork
2 green onions (including tops), thinly sliced
1 tablespoon chopped cilantro (Chinese parsley)
2 teaspoons minced ginger
2 tablespoons soy sauce
1 tablespoon dry sherry or Chinese rice wine
1 tablespoon sesame oil
2 teaspoons cornstarch
½ teaspoon black pepper
2 teaspoons vegetable oil

Spiced with ginger, fresh cilantro, and green onion, these sausage patties make the perfect partner to breakfast eggs. If time permits, season the meat and then chill it overnight so the flavors have time to blend.

Serves 4

1. Combine all the ingredients except the oil in a large bowl. Mix well and shape into eight patties, each about 2½ inches in diameter.

2. Place a wide frying pan over medium heat until hot. Add the oil, swirling to coat the surface. Add the sausage patties; cook for 2 minutes on each side or until lightly browned. Cover and cook for 2 more minutes, then uncover. Cook until the patties are no longer pink in the center, about 2 more minutes on each side.

VARIATION: For a reduced-calorie version, use ground turkey in place of the pork.

Chinese Sausage (Lop Cheong)

2¼ pounds pork butt
¾ pound pork back fat
3 tablespoons (packed) brown sugar
2 teaspoons salt
2 tablespoons soy sauce
1 tablespoon sweet sherry
3 tablespoons Scotch whiskey
1 teaspoon Chinese five-spice
2 tablespoons water
Hog casings

Small, slightly sweet and spicy Chinese sausages are used in many of the recipes in this book. If you cannot get them, here is a recipe for making your own. It comes from San Francisco sausage maker Bruce Aidells, whose sausage making workshops are always a hit at my cooking school.

Makes 6 sausages, about 2 ounces each

1. Grind the pork and fat in a meat grinder fitted with a ⅜-inch plate or, to be more authentic, dice the meat and fat with a knife into ¼-inch cubes. Combine all the remaining ingredients except the casings in a large mixing bowl. Add the meat and fat and mix well.

2. Stuff the meat mixture into the hog casing; tie the casing

into 5-inch links. Prick the links all over with a fork. Spread them on a rack and place them in the refrigerator. Let the sausages dry overnight.

3. Preheat the oven to 200°. Place the sausages on a rack in a foil-lined baking sheet, making sure they do not touch each other. Bake for 5 hours. Shut off the oven but do not open the oven door. Let the sausages cool for another 2 hours. Discard any excess fat in the pan and store the sausages in the refrigerator for one to two weeks, or freeze them for two to three months.

Thai Pork and Basil Stir-Fry

2 tablespoons vegetable oil
1 tablespoon minced garlic
2 or 3 serrano or jalapeño chiles, seeded and slivered
¾ pound boneless pork, thinly sliced
½ cup fresh basil leaves, cut into fine shreds
2 green onions (including tops), cut into 1½-inch pieces
2 tablespoons chicken broth or water
1½ tablespoons fish sauce
1 teaspoon sugar
1½ teaspoons cornstarch dissolved in 1 tablespoon water

Sometimes I like to give my Chinese stir-fry a peppery Thai accent. Here I use a flavorful combination of Thai fish sauce (*nam pla*), basil, and chile peppers. Try it—it's hot and sensational!

Serves 4

Place a wok or wide frying pan over high heat until hot. Add the oil, swirling to coat the sides. Add the garlic and chiles and cook, stirring, until fragrant, about 10 seconds. Add the pork and stir-fry until it is no longer pink, about 2½ minutes. Add the basil and green onions and stir-fry for 30 seconds. Add the broth, fish sauce, and sugar; mix well and add the cornstarch solution. Cook, stirring, until the sauce boils and thickens.

TIPS: You can adjust the amount of chile to achieve the degree of hotness you like.

If you can find it, try using Thai basil, which has a stronger anise flavor than regular basil.

Succulent Stuffed Pork

Marinade
2 tablespoons soy sauce
2 tablespoons dry sherry or
Chinese rice wine
½ teaspoon Chinese five-spice

❀

1 boneless pork loin roast
(about 2½ pounds),
butterflied (see Note)
1 Chinese sausage
(about 2 ounces),
cut into ¼-inch cubes
1 medium onion,
coarsely chopped
1 green onion (including
top), thinly sliced
1 bunch (8 to 10 ounces)
mustard greens or
Swiss chard, chopped
½ cup diced water chestnuts
2 tablespoons soy sauce
1 tablespoon rice vinegar
½ teaspoon black pepper
1 teaspoon cornstarch
1 tablespoon hoisin sauce

If you're looking for something special, you've turned to the right page. Tender pork and a flavorful stuffing of Chinese sausage, greens, and seasonings create a magnificent roast pork entree.

Serves 6

1. Combine the marinade ingredients in a small bowl and rub over the pork. Let stand for 20 minutes.

2. Place a wok or wide frying pan over high heat until hot. Add the sausage and cook for 1 minute. Add the onion and green onion and cook for 1 minute. Add the mustard greens, water chestnuts, soy sauce, vinegar, and pepper and cook until the greens are wilted, about 2 minutes. Add the cornstarch; mix well and let cool.

3. Preheat the oven to 350°. Spread the hoisin sauce over the open surface of the pork, then spread the stuffing evenly to within one inch of the edge. Roll the roast tightly and secure it with string, tying it once lengthwise then crosswise at 2-inch intervals. Place the roast on a rack in a large foil-lined baking pan. Bake uncovered to an internal temperature of 155°, about 1½ hours. Remove the roast from the oven and let it stand for at least 10 minutes before cutting it into thin slices (the internal temperature will rise to 165°).

VARIATION: The roast can also be braised in a wok. Brown the surface first in a little oil, add chicken broth or Master Sauce (see page 103) to a depth of 1 inch, cover, and simmer for 1½ hours, or until the internal temperature reaches 165°.

NOTE: To butterfly a pork loin roast, split it in half horizontally, almost all the way through, leaving one long edge attached, and unfold the halves like the wings of a butterfly. Ask your butcher to butterfly it for you if you like.

Tomato Beef

Marinade

2 tablespoons soy sauce
2 tablespoons dry sherry or
  Chinese rice wine
2 teaspoons cornstarch

✿

¾ pound flank steak, thinly
  sliced across the grain

Sauce

⅓ cup chicken broth
¼ cup catsup
1 tablespoon soy sauce
1 tablespoon distilled
  white vinegar
1 teaspoon hot pepper sauce
1 teaspoon sesame oil
2 teaspoons sugar

✿

3 tablespoons vegetable oil
1 teaspoon minced garlic
1 small onion, cut into
  1-inch squares
1 small green bell pepper,
  seeded and cut into
  1-inch squares
2 medium tomatoes, each
  cut into 8 wedges
2½ teaspoons cornstarch
  dissolved in
  2 tablespoons water

This is such a popular dish in most Chinese restaurants, I think of it as a blue plate special. It cooks in a flash, and the combination of beef, vegetables, and my secret sauce makes it a good choice for an easy one-dish entree to serve with rice or noodles.

Serves 4 to 6

1. Combine the marinade ingredients in a medium bowl. Add the beef, stir to coat, and set aside for 30 minutes. Combine the sauce ingredients in a small bowl; set aside.

2. Place a wok or wide frying pan over high heat until hot. Add 2 tablespoons of the vegetable oil, swirling to coat the sides. Add the beef and stir-fry until barely pink, about 2 minutes. Remove the beef from the wok and add the remaining tablespoon of oil. Add the garlic and onion and cook until the onion is soft and translucent, about 1 minute. Add the bell pepper; stir for 30 seconds. Stir in the tomatoes and the sauce mixture and mix well. Return the beef to the wok and add the cornstarch solution. Cook, stirring, until the sauce boils and thickens.

TIP: If you wish to peel the tomatoes before cutting them into wedges, dip them in boiling water for 15 to 30 seconds, plunge them into cold water to cool, then pull off the skin in strips.

96

My Mom's Ginger Beef

Marinade

1 tablespoon soy sauce
2 tablespoons dry sherry or Chinese rice wine
2 teaspoons vegetable oil
2 teaspoons cornstarch

❀

¾ pound beef sirloin or flank steak, thinly sliced across the grain

Sauce

¼ cup chicken broth
1 tablespoon dry sherry or Chinese rice wine
3 tablespoons oyster sauce
¼ teaspoon white pepper
1½ teaspoons cornstarch

❀

3 tablespoons vegetable oil
¼ cup slivered young ginger
3 green onions (including tops), cut into 1-inch pieces
2 tablespoons finely shredded pickled ginger

The list of curative powers credited to fresh ginger is as long as a Chinese scroll. It's reputed to aid digestion, prevent colds, restore appetite, and make a young (or old) man aware of the pleasures of spring. You seldom find beef this gingery in a restaurant. My Mom made it this way, not to stimulate my appetite but to soothe it.

Serves 4

1. Combine the marinade ingredients in a medium bowl. Add the beef and stir to coat. Set aside for 30 minutes. Combine the sauce ingredients in a small bowl.

2. Place a wok or wide frying pan over high heat until hot. Add 2 tablespoons of the oil, swirling to coat the sides. Add the beef and stir-fry until barely pink, about 2 minutes. Remove the beef from the wok. Add the remaining tablespoon of oil. Add the ginger and green onions and cook, stirring, for 1 minute. Return the beef to the wok. Add the pickled ginger and sauce. Cook, stirring, until the sauce boils and thickens.

TIP: Some cooks don't peel carrots, and some cooks don't peel ginger. I peel ginger because it makes a dish look more refined. Young ginger, however, need only be washed. The skin is thin and translucent.

Fragrant Beef and Vegetable Stew

Marinade
1 tablespoon soy sauce
½ teaspoon sesame oil
½ teaspoon sugar

❀

2 pounds beef shank
2-inch strip dried tangerine
    peel
2 whole star anise
½ teaspoon whole cloves
½ teaspoon fennel seeds
1 tablespoon vegetable oil
4 cloves garlic,
    lightly crushed
2 thick slices ginger,
    lightly crushed
1 can (14½ ounces)
    or 2 cups beef broth
¼ cup dry sherry or
    Chinese rice wine
3 tablespoons soy sauce
1 tablespoon hoisin sauce
2 teaspoons sugar
1½ pounds daikon, cut
    into 1-inch chunks
2 green onions (including
    tops), cut into 2-inch
    pieces
1 large carrot, cut into
    1-inch chunks
2 tablespoons cornstarch
    dissolved in ¼ cup water
½ teaspoon sesame oil
Hot cooked rice or noodles

Every country has its classic one-pot recipes which are handed down from one generation of cooks to the next, and China is no exception. We love their homespun flavors and their ease of preparation. One of my favorites includes beef, carrot, and the giant white radish, daikon, cooked in a faintly sweet, spiced gravy. It's the perfect partner to rice or noodles.

Serves 6

1. Combine the marinade ingredients in a medium bowl. Cut off and discard the skin from the beef shanks. Bone the shanks, reserving the bones. Cut the meat into 2-inch chunks and add it to the marinade, stirring to coat. Let stand for 30 minutes. Soak the tangerine peel in warm water to cover for 30 minutes; drain. Tie up the tangerine peel, star anise, cloves, and fennel seeds in a square of cheesecloth.

2. Place a large pot over high heat until hot. Add the vegetable oil, swirling to coat the surface. Add the garlic and ginger and cook, stirring, until fragrant, about 10 seconds. Add the beef and cook until lightly browned, about 2 minutes. Add the reserved bones, the spice bag, broth, sherry, soy sauce, hoisin sauce, and sugar. Stir to mix evenly. Add the daikon and green onions and bring to a boil. Reduce the heat to low, cover and simmer for 45 minutes. Add the carrot and continue to cook until the meat is tender when pierced, about 45 more minutes. Discard the spice bag and bones. Add the cornstarch solution and cook, stirring, until the sauce boils and thickens. Stir in the sesame oil. Serve over rice or noodles.

TIP: Daikon is the Japanese name for a large, cylindrical white radish up to 1½ feet long and 2 inches in diameter; it is also known as a Chinese white turnip or Korean turnip. Japan's most important vegetable, it is a staple in Chinese cooking as well. The Chinese variety is shorter, thicker, and more fibrous than the Japanese, and has a stronger flavor.

Grilled Steak with Black Mushrooms

1½ pounds New York strip, porterhouse, or other tender beef steak, cut about 1 inch thick

Marinade

1 tablespoon minced ginger
1 teaspoon toasted Sichuan peppercorns, ground (see page 17)
¼ cup soy sauce
3 tablespoons dry sherry or Chinese rice wine
1 teaspoon black pepper

❀

8 to 10 dried black mushrooms, or fresh shiitake mushrooms, sliced

Sauce

½ cup beef broth
2 tablespoons oyster sauce
1 tablespoon dry sherry or Chinese rice wine
2 teaspoons Worcestershire sauce
1 teaspoon sesame oil
1½ teaspoons cornstarch

❀

2 tablespoons butter or margarine
1 tablespoon minced shallots
2 teaspoons minced garlic
2 teaspoons minced ginger

You may not choose to eat this steak with chopsticks like I do, but even if you're going to eat it with a fork, follow the traditional Chinese style and cut the meat into thin strips before smothering it with the succulent black mushroom sauce.

Serves 4

1. Score the beef lightly on each side with shallow crisscross marks. Combine the marinade ingredients in a sealable plastic bag. Add the beef, seal the bag, and turn it a couple of times to evenly coat the meat. Refrigerate overnight.

2. If using dried black mushrooms, soak them in warm water to cover for 30 minutes; drain. Cut off and discard the stems and thinly slice the caps. (Fresh mushrooms can be sliced stem and all.) Set aside.

3. Combine the sauce ingredients in a small bowl; set aside. Lift the beef from the marinade and grill it on a lightly greased grill over a solid bed of low-glowing coals for 4 minutes. Turn and continue to cook until it is done to your liking, 4 more minutes for medium rare.

4. While the steak cooks, melt the butter in a small frying pan over medium heat. Add the shallots, garlic, and ginger and cook, stirring, until fragrant, about 10 seconds. Add the mushrooms and cook until tender, about 2 minutes. Add the sauce mixture and cook, stirring, until the sauce boils and thickens. Carve the steak into ½-inch-thick slices and top with the mushroom sauce.

VARIATION: The steak can also be broiled 2 inches from the heat, or cooked in a ridged grilling pan.

Teriyaki Beef with Rainbow Vegetables

2 teaspoons minced garlic
1 pound tender boneless
   beef such as sirloin,
   about
   ½ inch thick
½ teaspoon black pepper

Teriyaki Sauce
2 teaspoons minced ginger
½ cup sake (Japanese rice
   wine)
⅓ cup soy sauce
¼ cup sugar
1 tablespoon cornstarch
   dissolved in
   2 tablespoons water
❀
2 tablespoons vegetable oil
1 teaspoon minced ginger
1 small onion, cut into
   1-inch squares
1½ cups broccoli florets
1½ cups cauliflower florets
1 small carrot, thinly
   sliced diagonally
½ cup chicken broth
½ cup sliced fresh
   mushrooms
2 teaspoons soy sauce
⅛ teaspoon black pepper
1 teaspoon cornstarch
   dissolved in
   2 teaspoons water

This Japanese-style dish is quick, easy, and so delicious that I like to fix it even when I'm not pressed for time. The textures and colors of the vegetables contrast nicely with the succulent beef and its slightly sweet sauce. Try the same vegetables as a side dish with any other simply cooked meat dish.

Serves 4

1. Rub half the garlic onto the beef; sprinkle with pepper and set aside for 30 minutes.

2. Combine the teriyaki sauce ingredients in a small saucepan; cook, stirring constantly, over medium heat until the sauce boils and thickens. Remove from the heat; cover the pan to keep the sauce warm.

3. Place a wide frying pan over medium-high heat until hot. Add 1 tablespoon of the oil, swirling to coat the surface. Add the beef and cook until done to your liking, 2 minutes per side for medium rare. Remove the beef from the pan and keep it warm. Heat the remaining tablespoon of oil in the pan until hot. Add the remaining garlic, ginger, and onion; cook, stirring, until the onion softens. Add the broccoli, cauliflower, carrot, and broth; cover and cook for 2 minutes. Add the mushrooms and cook until the broccoli, cauliflower, and carrot are crisp-tender, about 1 more minute. Stir in the soy sauce and pepper and add the cornstarch solution. Cook, stirring, until the sauce boils and thickens. To serve, slice the beef diagonally into ¼-inch-thick slices, pour the sauce over the slices, and serve with the vegetables on the side.

TIP: To save time, pre-cut vegetables can be purchased at many supermarket salad bars.

Lamb

In Chinese cooking, lamb is almost always associated with the cooking of the northwestern regions. The arid plains of Mongolia and northwestern China are better suited to herding sheep than raising crops, and lamb and mutton are the most common meats there. Many Chinese from other regions find its flavor too strong, but I have learned to like it cooked in many ways, including "red-cooked," the Shanghai-style method usually reserved for other meats and poultry.

Hoisin Lamb Kabobs

Marinade

1 teaspoon minced garlic
2 tablespoons hoisin sauce
1 tablespoon catsup
1 tablespoon dry sherry or
   Chinese rice wine
1 tablespoon soy sauce
½ teaspoon hot pepper
   sauce or chili oil

✿

¼ pound boneless lamb sirloin,
   cut across the grain into
   3 strips, each 3 inches long,
   1 inch wide, and
   ¼ inch thick
3 bamboo skewers, soaked in
   water for 30 minutes
1 zucchini or yellow
   crookneck squash,
   cut into 1-inch-thick rounds
½ red bell pepper, seeded
   and cut into 1-inch squares

I prepared this recipe for the show entitled "Cooking for One," thus the small quantity. But broiling is an easy, convenient, and healthful way to cook, whether for one or for twenty, so feel free to increase the recipe.

Serves 1

1. Combine the marinade ingredients in a medium bowl. Add the lamb, stirring to coat it evenly. Cover and refrigerate for 1 hour or overnight.

2. Remove the lamb from the marinade; reserve the marinade. On each skewer, thread 1 strip of lamb, accordion-style, with pieces of zucchini and bell pepper between the folds. Brush with the reserved marinade. Place the skewers on a rack in a foil-lined baking pan. Broil 2 to 3 inches from the heat, turning once and brushing occasionally with marinade until the lamb is done to your liking, about 7 minutes for medium rare.

Mongolian Lamb

Marinade

2 tablespoons dry sherry or
   Chinese rice wine
1 tablespoon soy sauce
1 teaspoon sesame oil
2 teaspoons cornstarch
½ teaspoon sugar
Pinch of Chinese
   five-spice

✿

¾ pound boneless lean lamb
   (leg or shoulder), thinly
   sliced

Sauce

¼ cup chicken broth
1½ tablespoons soy sauce
1 tablespoon dry sherry or
   Chinese rice wine
1 tablespoon rice vinegar
2 teaspoons sesame oil
½ teaspoon hot pepper
   sauce or chili oil
½ teaspoon sugar
1½ teaspoons cornstarch

✿

6 green onions
1 large or 2 medium leeks
   Vegetable oil for
   deep-frying
2 ounces dried bean thread
   noodles
8 to 10 whole dried chile
   peppers
8 thin slices ginger
4 cloves garlic, thinly sliced
¼ teaspoon ground toasted
   Sichuan peppercorns (see
   page 17)
½ teaspoon sugar

In northern China and Mongolia, summers are hot and winters are cold. Spicy dishes like this are popular all year, to warm up a wintry night or to give you a cooling glow on a hot summer day.

Serves 4

1. Combine the marinade ingredients in a medium bowl. Add the lamb and stir to coat. Let stand for 30 minutes. Combine the sauce ingredients in a small bowl.

2. Cut the green onions and leeks (including tops) into 2-inch pieces. Set a wok in a ring stand and add oil to a depth of about 2 inches. Place over high heat until the oil reaches 375°. Add half the bean thread noodles and deep-fry until they puff and expand, about 5 seconds. Turn over to cook the other side. Lift out and drain on paper towels. Cook the remaining noodles. Place the noodles on a serving platter and press down to flatten them slightly.

3. Remove all but 2 tablespoons of oil from the wok. Add the chiles and stir-fry for 10 seconds. Add the lamb and stir-fry until barely pink, about 2 minutes. Remove the lamb from the wok. Add 2 teaspoons of oil and the ginger and garlic to the wok and cook, stirring, until fragrant, about 10 seconds. Add the green onions, leeks, and peppercorns and cook for 1 minute. Add the sugar and cook for 30 seconds or until caramelized. Return the lamb to the wok. Add the sauce and cook, stirring, until the sauce boils and thickens. Serve over the noodles.

TIP: Bean thread noodles, known as *fun see* in Chinese, and in English as bean threads, cellophane noodles, or Chinese vermicelli, are thin, translucent noodles made from mung bean starch. They do not need to be boiled; to use them in soups or casseroles, just soak them in hot water until soft. Or deep-fry them as in this recipe for garnishing salads. To avoid a mess when separating a bundle of bean threads, do it inside a bag.

Red-Cooked Lamb

Sauce

2 tablespoons vegetable oil
4 cloves garlic, crushed
6 thin slices ginger
2 whole star anise
1 piece dried tangerine peel
 or 2 pieces fresh orange peel
 (white part removed),
 each about 1½ inches
 square
4 cups chicken broth
¼ cup regular soy sauce
¼ cup dry sherry or
 Chinese rice wine
⅓ cup dark soy sauce
3 tablespoons sugar

❀

3-pound piece lamb shoulder
¾ teaspoon cornstarch
 dissolved in
 1½ teaspoons water
Thinly sliced cucumber
 for garnish

Red-cooking, a technique from eastern China, gets its name from the beautiful red-brown color of meats simmered in a highly seasoned soy sauce. You can use the cooking liquid, or "master sauce," over and over again, and it gets richer each time you use it. Add a little water, broth, or fresh soy sauce and a bit of the seasonings each time you re-use the sauce to maintain the color and flavor.

Serves 4

1. Place a medium saucepan over high heat until hot. Add the oil, swirling to coat the sides. Add the garlic and ginger and cook, stirring, until fragrant, about 10 seconds. Add the remaining sauce ingredients and bring to a boil. Reduce the heat to low, cover, and simmer for 20 minutes.

2. Meanwhile, place the lamb in a pot just large enough to hold it snugly; cover it with cold water. Bring to a boil, cook for 4 minutes, and drain. Remove the lamb and rinse the pot. Return the lamb to the pot and add the sauce. (If necessary, add just enough chicken broth or water so the lamb is barely covered.) Bring to a boil. Reduce the heat and simmer, covered, until the lamb is tender when pierced, about 2 hours.

3. Pour off the sauce and strain it. Bring ½ cup of the sauce to a boil in a small saucepan. Add the cornstarch solution and cook, stirring, until the sauce boils and thickens. To serve, cut the lamb into very thin slices. Arrange them on a serving plate and garnish with sliced cucumber. Serve with the thickened sauce.

TIPS: Refrigerate the remaining sauce to use again. Lift any congealed fat off the sauce before using.

If you wish to serve the lamb thinly sliced as part of an appetizer cold plate, let it cool in the sauce.

Lamb Firepot

3 ounces bean threads

2 pounds boneless lamb (leg or loin), cut into thin strips

1 pound medium raw shrimp, shelled and deveined (optional)

1 bunch spinach (about ¾ pound), washed and drained, stems removed

2 green onions (including tops), cut into 1-inch pieces

8 cups chicken broth

1 slice ginger, crushed

2 tablespoons dry sherry or Chinese rice wine

Dipping Sauce #1:
Hot and Spicy Sauce

1 tablespoon minced ginger

1 tablespoon minced garlic

1 teaspoon chopped cilantro (Chinese parsley)

¼ cup chicken broth

2 tablespoons soy sauce

2 teaspoons chili paste

⅛ teaspoon white pepper

Dipping Sauce #2:
Sweet and Sour
Plum Sauce

⅓ cup plum sauce

2 tablespoons seasoned rice vinegar

1 tablespoon soy sauce

2 teaspoons sesame oil

A Mongolian hot pot is a handsome piece of equipment to use for communal table-top cooking. It consists of a cylindrical chimney that holds coals surrounded by a moat that holds liquid. The diners become cooks. They pick out a bite of food, cook it in the bubbly broth, then dip it in savory sauce before eating. If this sounds complicated, try lamb firepot in an electric wok and see how easy and delicious it can be. Serve it with your choice of two or three dipping sauces. After you are done with the meat, shrimp, vegetables, and noodles, serve the delicious broth as a soup.

Serves 6 to 8

1. Soak the bean threads in warm water to cover for 30 minutes. Drain and cut into 3-inch lengths. Place on a serving platter with the lamb, shrimp, spinach, and green onions. Cover and refrigerate until ready to cook.

2. Combine the dipping sauce ingredients in separate small serving bowls.

3. In a large pot, bring the broth, ginger, and sherry to a boil. Reduce the heat and simmer, covered, for 20 minutes. Discard the ginger. Set the Mongolian firepot or an electric wok in the center of the table. Arrange the meat, shrimp, vegetables, and dipping sauces around the cooking vessel. Pour the hot broth into the firepot and adjust the heat so the broth simmers gently. Each diner cooks his or her choice of ingredients and seasons it with a dipping sauce.

Dipping Sauce #3:
Hoisin-Flavored Sauce

3 tablespoons hoisin sauce
2 tablespoons chicken broth
1 tablespoon catsup
1 tablespoon soy sauce
2 teaspoons honey
1 teaspoon Worcestershire sauce

Dipping Sauce #4:
Tangy Mustard Sauce

1 tablespoon minced garlic
¼ cup chicken broth
3 tablespoons prepared Chinese mustard
2 tablespoons sesame oil
2 teaspoons soy sauce

Dipping Sauce #5:
Curry-Flavored Sauce

5 tablespoons canned unsweetened coconut milk
2 tablespoons soy sauce
2 tablespoons peanut butter
1 tablespoon curry powder
½ teaspoon Chinese five-spice
¼ teaspoon ground coriander
⅛ teaspoon ground cumin

Dipping Sauce #6:
Miso Sauce

2 tablespoons fresh lemon juice or rice vinegar
¼ teaspoon grated lemon peel
⅓ cup Japanese rice wine (sake)
¼ cup white miso
½ teaspoon sugar

Vegetables and Salads

Grilled Eggplant and Green Onions
Asian Vegetable Stew
Garlic Chive Omelet
Chinese Hash Browns
Spicy Leek and Jicama Stir-Fry
Wok-Braised Chinese Fungus
Braised Eggplant with Garlic Sauce
Chinese Cabbage Rolls
Chinese Cabbage in Clear Sauce
Gingered Yams
Kim Chee
Calamari with Chinese Vinaigrette
Spinach with Sesame Dressing
Thai Cucumber Salad
Chicken Salad with Glazed Walnuts
Asparagus with Spicy Sesame Vinaigrette
Chinese Coleslaw
Cold-Tossed Jellyfish
Chiang Mai Lettuce Cups (Larb)
Crisp Cucumbers with Tomatoes
Chinese-Style Potato Salad
Cabbage and Pear Salad

Vegetables and Salads

Vegetables are my favorite subject. Chinese dishes are naked without vegetables. Fresh vegetables (along with rice and noodles) are the foundation of the Chinese diet; when cooked lightly in the Chinese way they retain all their texture, color, flavor, and natural goodness. Overcooking vegetables is not only a sin, it is wasteful.

Nowadays, Asian and other exotic vegetables are more widely available than ever, and mail-order seeds put them in the reach of every home gardener. Can you think of another hobby that literally puts food on your table? Of course, not all the recipes here call for exotic vegetables; familiar Western favorites such as asparagus, eggplant, carrots, and potatoes are also at home in Chinese-style vegetable cookery.

Along with the traditional vegetable dishes in this chapter are an assortment of "salads." You won't find vegetable salads in a normal Chinese meal; in fact, raw vegetables are rare in Chinese cooking, though they are popular in many other Asian cuisines. But we do enjoy plenty of "cold-tossed" dishes consisting of cool or room-temperature vegetables and sometimes meat, poultry, or seafood in a dressing.

Grilled Eggplant and Green Onions

Marinade
1 tablespoon minced garlic
2 tablespoons soy sauce
1 tablespoon Chinese dark
  rice vinegar or balsamic
  vinegar
1 tablespoon vegetable oil
2 teaspoons sesame oil

❀

4 Asian eggplants,
  each about 6 inches long
8 green onions
  (including tops)
1 tablespoon Chinese dark
  rice vinegar or balsamic
  vinegar

I like making things easy. That's why when I cook outdoors I often grill vegetables along with the main course. Marinated eggplant "fans" and green onions cook quickly over low-glowing coals, and the grilled flavor is fantastic.

Serves 4

1. Combine the marinade ingredients in a 9- by 13-inch baking dish. Cut the eggplants lengthwise into ¼-inch-thick slices, cutting up to but not through the stem ends. Gently spread them open to make fan shapes. Trim the root ends of the green onions. Cut the tops so each onion is 6 to 8 inches long; slash the white part. Place the eggplants and onions in the pan with the marinade; brush marinade over all the cut surfaces of the vegetables. Let stand for 10 minutes.

2. Spread the eggplant fans out on an oiled grill 3 to 4 inches above a solid bed of low-glowing coals. Cook until they are soft, 2 to 3 minutes on each side. Cook the green onions for about 1 minute on each side. Arrange the grilled vegetables on a platter and sprinkle with vinegar.

TIP: You can broil these flavorful vegetables indoors if you prefer.

111

Asian Vegetable Stew

6 dried black mushrooms

Sauce
¼ cup chicken broth
¼ cup dry sherry or
    Chinese rice wine
3 tablespoons soy sauce
1 teaspoon chili paste
1 teaspoon sesame oil
½ teaspoon black pepper

✿

1 medium leek (white part
    only), trimmed
3 Asian or 1 regular eggplant
    (about 1 pound)
3 medium tomatoes, peeled
1 small red bell pepper, seeded
3 small zucchini (about 1
    pound)
3 tablespoons vegetable oil
6 large cloves garlic,
    lightly mashed
4 slices ginger,
    lightly mashed
¼ pound pearl onions
    OR 1 small onion,
    coarsely chopped
2 teaspoons cornstarch
    dissolved in
    4 teaspoons water
2 teaspoons sesame oil

Although this really is a stew, it probably deserves a fancier name. It's a delicious mixture of summer vegetables, similar to the French dish ratatouille, that I season with Chinese flavorings. Serve it hot or at room temperature. If you happen to have any left over, use it as a filling for omelets.

Serves 8

1. Soak the mushrooms in warm water to cover for 30 minutes; drain. Cut off and discard the stems and cut the caps in half. Combine the sauce ingredients in a small bowl; set aside.

2. Cut the leek, eggplant, and tomatoes into 1-inch chunks. Cut the bell pepper into 1-inch squares. Cut the zucchini into ½-inch-thick slices.

3. Place a large pot over high heat until hot. Add the vegetable oil, swirling to coat the pan. Add the garlic, ginger, and onions and cook, stirring, for 1 minute. Add the leek and cook for 1 minute. Add the eggplant and cook for 2 minutes. Add the mushrooms, bell pepper, zucchini, tomatoes, and sauce; mix well. Bring to a boil; reduce the heat, cover, and simmer until all the vegetables are tender, about 20 minutes.

4. Add the cornstarch solution and cook, stirring, until the sauce boils and thickens. Stir in the sesame oil just before serving.

Garlic Chive Omelet

4 eggs
1 tablespoon chicken broth or water
½ teaspoon salt
¼ teaspoon white pepper
½ small onion, thinly sliced
½ teaspoon minced ginger
½ cup Chinese chives, cut into 1-inch pieces
½ cup finely shredded jicama
¼ pound cooked crabmeat, flaked, OR small cooked shrimp OR diced barbecued pork
1 tablespoon vegetable oil

Because I live in sunny California, Chinese chives grow vigorously in my garden and, with no effort on my part, re-seed themselves every year. I love their subtle, delicate garlic flavor, especially with eggs. If you're not a backyard farmer, look for the flat chives (*gow choy*) in Asian markets in late fall or early winter, or substitute regular chives for a more delicate flavor.

Serves 2 to 4

1. In a bowl, beat the eggs with the chicken broth, salt, and pepper. Divide the onion, ginger, chives, jicama, and crabmeat into two equal portions.

2. Place a 7- to 8-inch nonstick omelet pan over medium-high heat until hot. Add 1½ teaspoons of the vegetable oil, swirling to coat the surface. Add one portion of the onion and ginger and cook for 30 seconds. Pour in half the egg mixture. As the edges begin to set, lift one side with a spatula and shake the pan to let the uncooked egg flow underneath. Sprinkle the omelet with one portion of chives, jicama, and crabmeat. Continue cooking until the egg is set to your liking. Fold the omelet in half and slide it onto a serving plate. Repeat to make a second omelet using the remaining 1½ teaspoons of oil and the remaining filling ingredients.

TIPS: If you use frozen or canned crabmeat, drain it well before flaking.

Delicately flavored, but stronger than regular chives, Chinese chives (or garlic chives) are a foot long and have flat, dark green leaves. They are commonly used with eggs, in stir-fries, and with noodles. In Chinese markets you can also find yellow chives which are grown under cover to prevent them from developing a dark green color. They are sweeter, with a more delicate flavor and less fibrous texture, and are often used in soups. Flowering chives are also available in Asian stores. They are firm and crunchy, with round stalks.

113

Chinese Hash Browns

1 pound thin-skinned potatoes, cut into ½-inch cubes
2 tablespoons vegetable oil
1 Chinese sausage (about 2 ounces), cut into ¼-inch cubes
1 teaspoon minced garlic
¼ cup diced bamboo shoots
½ green bell pepper, seeded and cut into ½-inch squares
¼ teaspoon black pepper
1 tablespoon soy sauce
1 teaspoon sesame oil

What are breakfast eggs without a side of hash browns? I like mine Chinese style—seasoned with *lop cheong,* the little sweet-savory Chinese sausages that are sold in pairs.

Serves 4

1. Place the potato cubes in a medium pot; barely cover them with cold water. Bring to a boil, reduce the heat, and simmer until the potatoes are just tender when pierced, about 8 minutes. Drain well.

2. Place a wide frying pan over high heat until hot. Add the vegetable oil, swirling to coat the surface. Add the sausage and garlic and cook for 30 seconds. Add the potatoes and cook for 3 minutes, stirring occasionally. Reduce the heat to medium. Add the bamboo shoots, bell pepper, and black pepper. Cook, stirring, until the potatoes are lightly browned, about 2 minutes, then stir in the soy sauce and sesame oil. Cook until heated through, about 1 minute.

TIP: Because red and white thin-skinned potatoes (also called new potatoes) are firm and waxy, they keep their shape better during frying than thick-skinned russet potatoes.

If cooking the potatoes ahead of time, rinse them under cold water and drain them well before frying.

MICROWAVE METHOD: Cut the potatoes into ½-inch cubes, arrange them in a 9-inch microwave-safe glass pie pan, and sprinkle them with water. Cover and cook on high until tender, 4 to 5 minutes.

Spicy Leek and Jicama Stir-Fry

Sauce

2 tablespoons soy sauce
1 tablespoon dry sherry or
   Chinese rice wine
1 teaspoon sesame oil
Pinch of white pepper

✿

1 tablespoon vegetable oil
2 teaspoons minced ginger
6 whole dried chile peppers
2 leeks (white part only),
   cut into 1½-inch slivers
½ pound jicama, peeled and
   cut into matchstick pieces
1 carrot, cut into thin
   matchstick pieces
¼ cup chicken broth
1 teaspoon cornstarch
   dissolved in
   2 teaspoons water

I think someone should create a national jicama week. It is a terrific vegetable, both tasty and versatile. It retains its snowy white color, crisp texture, and sweet flavor when stir-fried and doesn't wilt or become watery when used raw in salads. I always buy the largest jicama I can find. It keeps up to a week, though in my kitchen it disappears long before that.

Serves 4

1. Combine the sauce ingredients in a small bowl.

2. Place a wok or wide frying pan over high heat until hot. Add the vegetable oil, swirling to coat the sides. Add the ginger and chile peppers and cook, stirring, until fragrant, about 10 seconds. Add the leeks and cook for 30 seconds. Add the jicama, carrot, and broth. Cover and cook until the carrot is crisp-tender, about 2 minutes. Stir in the sauce. Add the cornstarch solution and cook, stirring, until the sauce boils and thickens.

TIP: Dirt hides between the layers of leeks. To prepare them for cooking, trim the roots and tops, leaving about 3 inches of green leaves. Cut the leeks in half lengthwise, then wash them under running water, separating the layers to rinse out the dirt.

Wok-Braised Chinese Fungus

½ ounce dried white fungus
   (snow fungus)
½ ounce dried black fungus
   (cloud ear)
12 dried black mushrooms

Sauce
½ cup chicken broth
2 tablespoons oyster sauce
1 tablespoon dry sherry or
   Chinese rice wine
1 teaspoon soy sauce

✿

8 Chinese (napa) cabbage
   leaves for garnish
1 tablespoon vegetable oil
1 teaspoon minced ginger
½ cup canned gingko nuts,
   drained
2 teaspoons cornstarch
   dissolved in
   4 teaspoons water

The location of prime fungus hunting grounds in China is a secret as closely guarded as the whereabouts of truffle hunting areas in Italy. Don't worry. You can buy all three kinds of fungus, including succulent dried black mushrooms, in your local Chinese market. This typical Chinese dish is prized for its texture as well as its flavor.

Serves 6

1. Soak the white and black fungus and mushrooms in separate bowls in warm water to cover for 30 minutes; drain. Rinse the white fungus well to remove sand around the stems. Cut off and discard the mushroom stems. Combine the sauce ingredients in a small bowl.

2. Cook the cabbage leaves in a large pot of boiling water for 1 minute and drain well. Arrange on a serving platter.

3. Place a wok or wide frying pan over high heat until hot. Add the vegetable oil, swirling to coat the sides. Add the ginger and cook, stirring, until fragrant, about 10 seconds. Add the white and black fungus, mushrooms, gingko nuts, and sauce; mix well. Cover and simmer over medium-low heat for 10 minutes. Add the cornstarch solution and cook, stirring, until the sauce boils and thickens. Serve over the cabbage leaves.

TIPS: For extra contrast in texture, you can add a small can of sliced water chestnuts or sliced bamboo shoots.

Dried white fungus, also known as white tree fungus, snow ears, or silver fungus, have a spongy look in the dried state. After soaking, they are soft and almost translucent.

There are two common varieties of black fungus available in markets. Cloud ears are smaller and softer when soaked; wood ears are larger and firmer. They are sold dried, for the most part, for their medicinal properties (they're believed to prevent blood clots) as well as for cooking. Crumpled-looking, they have little flavor but a pleasant crunch.

Braised Eggplant with Garlic Sauce

4 Asian eggplants or
  1 large regular eggplant
  (about 1¼ pounds)
2 teaspoons salt

Sauce
¾ cup chicken broth
2 tablespoons soy sauce
1 tablespoon dry sherry or
  Chinese rice wine
1 tablespoon balsamic vinegar
  or dark Chinese rice vinegar
2 teaspoons sesame oil
2 teaspoons hoisin sauce
2 teaspoons chili paste

✿

2 tablespoons vegetable oil
¼ pound coarsely chopped
  boneless pork
1 tablespoon minced garlic
1 teaspoon minced ginger
2 green onions (including
  tops), thinly sliced
2 tablespoons coarsely
  chopped water chestnuts
2 teaspoons cornstarch
  dissolved in
  4 teaspoons water
Slivered green onion
  (including top) for
  garnish

Here's a chance to practice your skill with a cleaver. Although you can make this garlicky dish from Sichuan with ground pork, I prefer chopped pork for its more pleasing texture contrast to the creamy eggplant. Still, if you want to use your food processor, by all means do so.

Serves 4

1. Peel the eggplant and cut it into ½-inch cubes. Place it in a medium bowl, sprinkle with salt, and toss gently to mix. Set aside for 30 minutes.

2. Combine the sauce ingredients in a medium bowl. Drain and rinse the eggplant and squeeze it dry.

3. Place a wok or wide frying pan over high heat until hot. Add the vegetable oil, swirling to coat the sides. Add the pork and cook until browned and crumbly, about 1½ minutes. Add the garlic and ginger and cook, stirring, until fragrant, about 10 seconds. Add the eggplant, green onions, and water chestnuts; mix well. Add the sauce. Reduce the heat to medium, cover the pan and braise until the eggplant is tender and the liquid is slightly reduced, about 10 minutes. Add the cornstarch solution and cook, stirring, until the sauce boils and thickens. Garnish with slivered green onion.

TIP: Asian eggplant has a tender skin which does not require peeling. Do so only if you want the color of the dish to be light rather than tinged with purple.

Chinese Cabbage Rolls

½ pound ground turkey

Marinade
1 tablespoon soy sauce
1 tablespoon dry sherry or
  Chinese rice wine
1 tablespoon cornstarch

Stuffing
4 dried black mushrooms
1 small carrot, grated
2 green onions (including
  tops), thinly sliced
⅓ cup coarsely chopped
  water chestnuts
1 egg white, lightly beaten
2 teaspoons sesame oil
½ teaspoon sugar
¼ teaspoon white pepper

Sauce
⅔ cup vegetable juice
  cocktail
⅓ cup chicken broth
2 tablespoons rice vinegar
1 tablespoon soy sauce
¼ teaspoon white pepper

❀

8 large Chinese (napa)
  cabbage leaves
1 tablespoon vegetable oil
2 teaspoons minced garlic
2 teaspoons minced ginger
1½ teaspoons cornstarch
  dissolved in
  1 tablespoon water
1 green onion (including
  top), thinly sliced
Cooked brown rice (hot)

Let the cabbage roll! Each country has a version of this homey dish. What makes this Chinese? The Chinese (napa) cabbage—and the marinade and stuffing made with typical Chinese ingredients.

Makes 8

1. Combine the turkey and marinade ingredients in a large bowl; mix well, cover, and refrigerate for 30 minutes. Soak the mushrooms in warm water to cover for 30 minutes; drain. Cut off and discard the stems and coarsely chop the caps. Add the mushrooms and the remaining stuffing ingredients to the turkey, mix well, and set aside. Combine the sauce ingredients in a small bowl; set aside.

2. Cook the cabbage leaves in a large pot of boiling water until they are limp, about 2 minutes. Drain, rinse under cold running water, and drain again. To stuff each leaf, mound ⅛ of the stuffing at the stem end, fold the bottom of the leaf over the stuffing, then fold over the right and left sides; roll the whole package over once to enclose the stuffing.

3. Place a 10-inch frying pan over high heat until hot. Add the vegetable oil, swirling to coat the bottom of the pan. Add the garlic and ginger; cook, stirring, until fragrant, about 10 seconds. Remove the pan from the heat and arrange the cabbage rolls seam side down in a single layer in the pan. Pour the sauce over the rolls. Return the pan to medium-low heat; cover and simmer for 25 minutes.

4. Lift the rolls out with a slotted spoon and transfer them to a serving platter. Add the cornstarch solution to the pan juices; cook, stirring, until the sauce boils and thickens. Pour the sauce over the rolls and sprinkle with green onion. Serve with hot brown rice.

TIP: You can use lean ground beef or chicken in place of the turkey.

119

Chinese Cabbage in Clear Sauce

Broth Mixture
⅔ cup chicken broth
2 tablespoons dry sherry or Chinese rice wine
¾ teaspoon salt
¼ teaspoon white pepper
1½ teaspoons sugar
2 teaspoons sesame oil

❀

2 teaspoons vegetable oil
2 teaspoons minced ginger
2 teaspoons minced garlic
1 tablespoon cornstarch dissolved in
2 tablespoons water
1 head (about 2 pounds) Chinese (napa) cabbage, cored and cut lengthwise into 6 sections

Clear sauce is the Chinese counterpart to basic white sauce used in Western-style cooking. It goes perfectly with white meat chicken, turkey breast, scallops, and such steamed vegetables as Chinese (napa) cabbage, baby bok choy, or Shanghai baby greens.

Serves 6

1. Combine the broth mixture ingredients in a small bowl.

2. Place a medium saucepan over high heat until hot. Add the vegetable oil, swirling to coat the surface. Add the ginger and garlic and cook, stirring, until fragrant, about 10 seconds. Add the broth mixture and bring to a boil. Add the cornstarch solution and cook, stirring, until the sauce boils and thickens. Keep warm.

3. In a large pot, bring 3 inches of water to a boil. Plunge the cabbage into the water and cook until crisp-tender, about 4 minutes. Drain well and place on a platter. Serve the sauce over the cabbage.

TIP: The cabbage can also be cooked in a microwave. Place in a microwave-safe dish, cover, and cook on high until crisp-tender, about 4 minutes.

Gingered Yams

Ginger and yams have a long history in Chinese cuisine. In primitive times, wild yams were dug from the forest during famines. The ancient Chinese believed that a bite of ginger a day kept the doctor away. Today in China, some yams and ginger are planted in the same beds. I don't know if this ginger-yam team will keep you young, but it will surely satisfy your appetite.

Serves 4

2 pounds yams, peeled and
  cut into 2-inch cubes
2 thin slices ginger, crushed
½ cup fresh orange juice
¼ cup sugar
2 tablespoons chopped
  crystallized ginger
Salt to taste

Place yams and ginger slices in a large pot with water to cover. Bring to a boil, reduce the heat, cover, and simmer until the yams are tender, about 30 minutes. Drain; discard the ginger. Place the hot yams, orange juice, and sugar in a food processor and process just until smooth. (Or mash the hot yams with a potato masher until only fine lumps remain, then add the orange juice and sugar and continue mashing until smooth.) Remove to a serving bowl, stir in the crystallized ginger, and add salt to taste. Serve warm.

Kim Chee

1 medium head Chinese
  (napa) cabbage (1½ to
  2 pounds)
4 teaspoons salt
6 cloves garlic, minced
3 green onions (including
  tops), minced
2 teaspoons minced ginger
¼ cup rice vinegar
2 tablespoons soy sauce
1 tablespoon sesame oil
2 teaspoons cayenne pepper
¾ teaspoon ground toasted
  Sichuan peppercorns
  (see page 17)
6 whole dried chile peppers

Kim chee is one of the treasures of Korean cooking; a Korean meal served without it would seem almost bland. The most popular vegetable for kim chee is Chinese (napa) cabbage, which is salted, mixed with spices, and allowed to ferment to the desired degree of tartness. Serve this spicy side dish in small portions, just as you would any pickled vegetable.

Makes 2½ to 3 cups

1. Cut the cabbage lengthwise into sections about 2 inches wide; remove the core. Cut each section crosswise into 2-inch lengths. Place the cabbage in a large bowl, sprinkle it with the salt, and toss to mix well. Cover with an inverted plate and weight it down with a heavy object, such as a large juice can or a 1-quart jar filled with water. Let stand for 30 minutes. Lightly rinse the cabbage under cold running water and drain. Squeeze it to extract most of the liquid.

2. Combine the remaining ingredients in a large bowl. Add the cabbage and mix well. Transfer the mixture to a glass bowl or crock. Cover with an inverted plate and weight down with a heavy object. Refrigerate for 4 days before eating.

121

Calamari with Chinese Vinaigrette

Dressing

1 teaspoon minced garlic
2 tablespoons rice vinegar
2 tablespoons sesame oil
1 tablespoon fresh
    lemon juice
1 teaspoon soy sauce
1 teaspoon hot pepper sauce
1 tablespoon sugar
½ teaspoon salt
⅛ teaspoon white pepper
⅛ teaspoon crushed red
    pepper

❀

1 pound small squid, cleaned,
    with tentacles separated
    and body cut into ¼-inch
    rings
2 ounces snow peas, ends
    and strings removed, cut
    in half diagonally
2 stalks celery, thinly
    sliced
½ small red onion,
    thinly sliced
½ cup sliced water chestnuts

The tenderness and flavor of squid remind me of abalone—at a fraction of the cost. Cook squid very briefly or for a very long time. Cooked in between, the flesh is tough and rubbery.

Serves 4

1. Combine the dressing ingredients in a small bowl and whisk until well blended; set aside.

2. Bring 4 inches of water to a boil in a medium saucepan. Add the squid, including the tentacles, and cook for 1 minute. Drain, rinse under cold running water, and drain again. Toss with 2 tablespoons of the dressing and set aside for 30 minutes.

3. Cook the snow peas in boiling water for 1 minute or until crisp-tender. Drain, rinse under cold running water, and drain again. Combine in a large salad bowl with the squid and the remaining ingredients. Stir the remaining dressing, add it to the salad, and toss to coat evenly.

TIP: Many fish markets sell small squid already cleaned. To do it yourself, grasp the tentacles and gently pull them away from the hood. Pull and discard the long clear quill from the hood. Squeeze out and discard the contents of the hood, then pull off the thin speckled membrane from the hood to expose the white meat. Rinse well inside and out. With a sharp knife, cut between the eyes and tentacles; discard the eyes and the material attached. Pop out and discard the hard beak in the center of the tentacles.

Spinach with Sesame Dressing

Dressing

3 tablespoons sesame seeds, toasted (see page 17)

2 cubes (about 1½ tablespoons) white fermented bean curd (*fu yu*)

1 tablespoon dry sherry or Chinese rice wine

1 tablespoon sugar

1 teaspoon instant bonito soup stock base (*hon-dashi*) mixed with ¼ cup hot water

¼ teaspoon crushed red pepper

⅛ teaspoon white pepper

❀

1½ pounds spinach or watercress

A mixed green salad you toss. My spinach salad, made Chinese style with cooked spinach, you squeeze. After eliminating the water from the spinach bunches, I cut them into logs and arrange them on a serving plate. Depending on my mood, I stack them like cordwood or stand the bundles on end.

Serves 4 to 6

1. Place 2½ tablespoons of the sesame seeds in a blender with the rest of the dressing ingredients and blend until smooth. Without trimming the roots and stems, wash the spinach in a large bowl of water; discard any wilted leaves.

2. Bring a large pot of water to a boil. Add the spinach and cook for 1 minute. Drain, rinse under cold running water, and drain again. Lay 2 or 3 bunches of spinach together on a work surface so they form a bundle about 1 inch in diameter; squeeze to remove as much water as possible. Trim and discard the root ends and cut each bundle into 2-inch lengths. Repeat with the remaining spinach. Arrange the cut bundles on a serving platter and pour the dressing on top. Sprinkle with the remaining sesame seeds.

TIP: Fermented bean curd is packed in jars in a thin liquid flavored with wine. It may have chiles added for color and flavor. Don't be put off by its very pungent odor; it is delicious in this dressing. Covered and refrigerated, a jar of *fu yu* will keep for a long time.

MICROWAVE METHOD: In step 2, spin the spinach dry in a plastic salad spinner. Cover the spinner with plastic wrap, place it right in the microwave, and cook on high for 4 minutes. Divide the spinach into three bundles; lay them on paper towels and squeeze them dry, forming 1-inch logs as above. Trim, cut, and dress as above.

Thai Cucumber Salad

Dressing

3 tablespoons fresh
   lime juice
1 tablespoon minced garlic
1 tablespoon chopped cilantro
   (Chinese parsley)
3 tablespoons fish sauce
1 tablespoon sesame oil
2 tablespoons sugar
½ teaspoon crushed
   red pepper

✿

1 English cucumber or
   1½ regular cucumbers,
   seeded if necessary and
   thinly sliced
1 small red onion,
   thinly sliced
½ red bell pepper,
   seeded and cut into
   matchstick pieces
¼ pound small cooked shrimp
1 tablespoon toasted
   sesame seeds or chopped
   toasted nuts (optional)

When I was a kid growing up in China, all I knew was Chinese food. Now I enjoy foods from other Asian countries as well. This typical Thai salad is as cool as a cucumber, yet peppery-sweet.

Serves 4

Combine the dressing ingredients in a small bowl and let stand 30 minutes. Combine the cucumber, onion, bell pepper, and shrimp in a large bowl. Both the salad and the dressing may be prepared up to 4 hours ahead and refrigerated, but do not combine until just before serving. Pour the dressing over the salad and toss well. Sprinkle with sesame seeds or chopped nuts if desired.

Chinese Chicken Salad with Glazed Walnuts

Dressing

¼ cup balsamic vinegar or
   Chinese dark rice vinegar
3 tablespoons sesame paste or
   peanut butter
3 tablespoons walnut oil
1 tablespoon sesame oil
2 tablespoons soy sauce
1 teaspoon hot pepper sauce
2 tablespoons sugar
½ teaspoon black pepper

Salad

4 cups shredded
   iceberg lettuce
2 cups shredded
   cooked chicken
1 small carrot,
   cut into matchstick pieces
½ cucumber, peeled, seeded,
   and cut into matchstick
   pieces
2 tablespoons chopped
   cilantro (Chinese parsley)
2 tablespoons finely
   shredded fresh basil

❀

Vegetable oil for deep-frying
12 wonton wrappers, cut
   into ¼-inch-wide strips
2 tablespoons walnut oil
2 tablespoons sugar
½ cup toasted walnut halves

There are as many variations of Chinese chicken salad as there are moves in a game of mah jong. Place your money on this one; it's a sure winner. The glazed walnuts are traditionally deep-fried, but you can make them with less fuss in just a tiny bit of oil. To be on the safe side, double the amount of walnuts; you may eat half of them for snacks by the time you serve the salad.

Serves 6 to 8

1. Combine the dressing ingredients in a small bowl and whisk until smooth. Combine the salad ingredients in a large bowl, cover, and refrigerate until ready to serve.

2. Set a wok in a ring stand and add oil to a depth of about 2 inches. Heat the oil to 360° and adjust the heat to medium-high. Fry the wonton strips until golden brown, about 15 seconds. Remove them with a skimmer and drain on paper towels.

3. Place a wide frying pan over medium heat until hot. Add the walnut oil, swirling to coat the surface. Add the sugar, stir until it dissolves, add the walnuts, and stir until the nuts are coated with caramelized sugar. Immediately transfer the walnuts to a foil-covered plate and separate them with two forks.

4. Just before serving, pour the dressing over the salad and toss to coat evenly. Serve the salad in a wide shallow bowl, surrounded with the wonton strips. Scatter the glazed walnuts over the top.

TING TING JAHE
TOP QUALITY GOOD TASTE
GINGER CANDY
戶資金，
種服務項目，
房屋貸款等
avings of A

Asparagus with Spicy Sesame Vinaigrette

Dressing
½ teaspoon toasted
  sesame seeds (see page 17)
⅛ teaspoon toasted
  Sichuan peppercorns,
  ground (see page 17)
2 tablespoons white
  wine vinegar
1 tablespoon vegetable oil
1 tablespoon sesame oil
1 tablespoon catsup
2 teaspoons soy sauce
1 teaspoon chili paste
1½ teaspoons sugar
⅛ teaspoon white pepper
✿
2 pounds asparagus

You can simmer, steam, or microwave the asparagus to make this chilled vegetable side dish. The secret is to cook it just to the crisp-tender stage so that when it is served with the sesame-spiked vinaigrette it will look as fresh as it did before cooking.

Serves 4

1. Combine the dressing ingredients in a small bowl and whisk until well blended. Set aside. Snap off the tough ends of the asparagus. Peel the stalks if desired.

2. In a wide frying pan, cook the asparagus in 1 inch of boiling water until crisp-tender, 2 to 4 minutes. Drain, rinse under cold running water, and drain again. Arrange on a serving platter, cover, and refrigerate until ready to serve. Just before serving, pour the dressing over the asparagus.

TIP: It doesn't take guesswork to tell which part of an asparagus spear is tough and should be discarded and which part is tender and should be saved. Hold one end of the asparagus spear in each hand and bend. It will snap apart at the tough–tender division.

Chinese Coleslaw

Dressing
⅓ cup mayonnaise
3 tablespoons rice vinegar
2 tablespoons soy sauce
1 tablespoon sesame oil
2 teaspoons sugar
½ teaspoon Chinese five-spice

I'll tell you a secret: I don't always use my cleaver for cutting. To make long, skinny shreds of daikon and carrot, it's faster to use the julienne disc of a food processor. You can also make fast work of this style of cutting with the French shredding and slicing tool called a *mandoline* or the fine blade of a Japanese grater.

Serves 6

Combine the dressing ingredients in a small bowl and whisk until evenly blended. Combine the salad ingredients in a large salad bowl. Just before serving, pour the dressing

Salad

5 cups shredded Chinese
  (napa) cabbage
1 cup daikon, cut into
  fine julienne
1 small carrot, cut into
  fine julienne
1 green onion (including
  top), cut into 1-inch slivers
2 tablespoons chopped
  cilantro (Chinese parsley)

over the salad and toss until evenly coated.

TIP: If you prefer a less nippy flavor, use jicama or sliced water chestnuts in place of the daikon. To build this salad into a main dish, toss in a generous handful of small cooked shrimp.

Cold-Tossed Jellyfish

1 package (1 pound)
  salted jellyfish

Sauce

1 tablespoon balsamic
  vinegar or Chinese dark
  rice vinegar
1 tablespoon soy sauce
1 teaspoon sesame oil
1 teaspoon toasted
  sesame seeds
½ teaspoon sugar
⅛ teaspoon white pepper

You'd think that by the time a jellyfish left the sea, it would have seen enough water! The recipe directions are correct. Wash the jellyfish for 15 minutes—30 if you have time. The more it is rinsed, the more crispy and crunchy it becomes.

Serves 6 as an appetizer

1. Without unfolding the layers, cut the jellyfish into very thin julienne strips, about 1/16-inch wide. Place the jellyfish in a colander and rinse it under cold running water for 15 minutes. Toss the jellyfish occasionally to rinse it evenly.

2. Bring a large pot of water to a boil and pour the hot water over the jellyfish. Immediately plunge the jellyfish in a large bowl of cold water and drain. Repeat the rinsing with boiling water and chilling with cold water one more time. Pat the jellyfish dry between paper towels. Combine the sauce ingredients in a medium bowl and add the jellyfish. Toss until evenly coated. Cover and refrigerate until ready to serve or for as long as one week.

Chiang Mai Lettuce Cups (Larb)

2 tablespoons uncooked rice
2 tablespoons vegetable oil
1 teaspoon crushed
   red pepper
2 tablespoons minced
   shallots
1 pound lean ground beef
3 green onions (including
   tops), thinly sliced
2 tablespoons chopped
   cilantro (Chinese parsley)
2 tablespoons chopped
   fresh mint leaves
¼ cup fresh lime juice
2 tablespoons fish sauce
1½ teaspoons sugar
Chilled romaine or
   butter lettuce leaves
Mint sprigs or lime
   wedges for garnish

When a cook prepares a dish from another cuisine, he invariably adds his own personal touch, and I've done so with this recipe. It's based on the *larb* of northern Thailand, in which the beef is eaten raw or blanched in water. I prefer to stir-fry it with seasonings to give it a Chinese accent.

Serves 4 to 6

1. Place a small frying pan over medium heat until hot. Add the rice; cook, shaking the pan frequently, until the rice is toasty brown, about 4 minutes. Let stand until cool. Place the rice in a spice grinder and grind to a fine powder.

2. Place a wok or wide frying pan over high heat until hot. Add the oil, swirling to coat the sides. Add the red pepper and shallots and cook, stirring, until the shallots soften, about 30 seconds. Add the beef and cook until it is browned and crumbly, about 3 minutes. Drain the excess liquid. Add the green onions, cilantro, mint, lime juice, fish sauce, and sugar; toss well. Add the ground rice and stir until the liquid is absorbed, about 30 seconds. To serve, mound the meat mixture on a platter and surround it with lettuce leaves. Garnish with mint sprigs. Serve warm or at room temperature. To eat, place a spoonful of meat in a lettuce leaf, wrap it up, and eat it out of hand.

131

Crisp Cucumbers with Tomatoes

Dressing

¼ cup seasoned rice vinegar
4 teaspoons sesame oil
½ teaspoon hot pepper sauce
Pinch of black pepper

❀

3 Japanese or 1 large English
   cucumber, thinly sliced
   (about 3 cups)
1 cup whole cherry or pear
   tomatoes, cut in half
1 green onion, thinly sliced
3 tablespoons toasted chopped
   walnuts

My father-in-law reads a seed catalog the way I read a cookbook. He can't wait to experiment with something new. His cucumbers are the best! I don't know if I prefer his Japanese variety or the pale green Armenian ones. If you can't find small thin-skinned cucumbers at your local farmer's market, I recommend the larger English variety for this crisp, cool salad.

Serves 4 to 6

Combine the dressing ingredients in a small bowl and whisk until smooth. Combine the remaining ingredients in a large bowl. Add the dressing and toss to coat evenly. Serve immediately.

Chinese-Style Potato Salad

1½ pounds thin-skinned
   potatoes

Dressing

½ cup mayonnaise
2 tablespoons soy sauce
2 tablespoons rice vinegar
1 teaspoon sesame oil
1 teaspoon prepared
   Chinese mustard
¾ teaspoon sugar
½ teaspoon salt

❀

There's American potato salad and German potato salad, so why not Chinese? I've had a great time adding Chinese flavorings to this summertime favorite. Who knows, maybe it will start a new tradition. Picnic anyone?

Serves 4

1. Place the potatoes in a pan with 1 inch of boiling water; cover and cook until tender when pierced, 20 to 25 minutes. Drain, cool slightly, peel, and cut into 1-inch cubes.

2. Whisk the dressing ingredients in a medium bowl; cover and refrigerate.

3. Place the potatoes in a large salad bowl with half the bacon and the bok choy, bell pepper squares, green

3 strips crisp bacon,
   crumbled
½ cup sliced bok choy stems
   or celery, cut into
   ¼-inch-thick slices
½ red bell pepper, seeded
   and cut into ¼-inch squares
2 green onions, thinly sliced
2 tablespoons chopped
   cilantro (Chinese parsley)
3 red bell pepper rings

onions, cilantro, and dressing. Toss to mix well. Garnish with the remaining bacon and the bell pepper rings. If made ahead, refrigerate until ready to serve. Refrigerate any leftovers.

MICROWAVE METHOD: In step 1, cut the potatoes into ½-inch cubes, arrange them in a 9-inch microwave-safe glass pie pan, and sprinkle them with water. Cover and cook on high until tender, 4 to 5 minutes.

Cabbage and Pear Salad

Dressing
2 teaspoons minced garlic
⅓ cup rice vinegar
3 tablespoons vegetable oil
1 tablespoon prepared
   Chinese mustard
2 tablespoons sesame oil
4 teaspoons sugar
1 teaspoon salt
❀
1 bunch watercress,
   tough stems removed
3 cups shredded cabbage
½ red bell pepper, seeded
   and cut into matchstick
   pieces
1 Asian pear or regular pear
   or red-skinned apple,
   unpeeled
2 teaspoons sesame seeds,
   toasted (see page 17)

Bursting with juice like a pear, but crisp like an apple, the Asian pear is usually sold ripe and ready to eat. There's no need to peel it before tossing it in this colorful salad.

Serves 6

Combine the dressing ingredients in a small bowl and whisk until evenly blended. Combine the watercress, cabbage, and bell pepper in a salad bowl; cover and refrigerate if not serving immediately. Just before serving, cut the pear into ½-inch cubes and add it to the salad bowl. Pour the dressing over the salad and toss until evenly coated. Sprinkle with sesame seeds.

VARIATION: Aromatic sesame oil gives this dressing a nutty flavor. Try it another time on a raw spinach salad.

Rice and Noodles

Rice and Noodles

The Chinese word for cooked rice, *fan,* is practically synonymous with the word for meal. When you ask a friend if he has eaten dinner, you literally ask him if he has eaten rice. While rice reigns over southern China, wheat is king up north. Northern Chinese dishes are often accompanied by noodles, buns, and dumplings. The noodles come in all shapes and textures; they can be made from rice or bean starch as well as from wheat. We Chinese are famous for using our noodles, in more ways than one.

Basic Chinese-Style Rice

1 cup long-grain rice
1½ cups cold water

For the slightly sticky type of rice served in Chinese restaurants, use long-grain (but never parboiled or converted) rice and add it to cold water. If you prefer it stickier, in the Japanese style, use a medium-grain variety; if you prefer more separate grains, bring the water to a boil first. When cooking a larger quantity of rice, allow 1½ cups water per additional cup of rice.

Makes 3 cups

Combine the rice and water in a medium saucepan. Bring to a boil, reduce the heat to medium-high, and cook uncovered until the water is nearly evaporated. Reduce the heat to low, cover, and simmer until the rice is tender, about 15 minutes. Remove from the heat and let stand, covered, for 5 minutes. Fluff with a fork before serving.

MICROWAVE METHOD: Combine 2 cups water and 1 cup rice in a 1½-quart microwave-safe bowl. Cover and cook on high for 5 minutes. Reduce the heat to medium and cook until the water is absorbed and the rice is fluffy, about 15 minutes.

Vegetable Fried Rice

Most Chinese do not eat brown rice; we get plenty of fiber in our diets from vegetables and fruits, and in the quantities in which we eat rice every day, using the whole grain would be too much. But brown rice is popular in the West, especially among vegetarians, so here's a way to use it along with assorted vegetables. Of course, you can add meat or seafood if you like.

Serves 6

- 2 tablespoons vegetable oil
- 2 teaspoons minced garlic
- 1 teaspoon minced ginger
- ½ small onion, cut into ¼-inch cubes
- 1 small carrot, cut into ¼-inch cubes
- 1 stalk celery, cut into ¼-inch cubes
- 2 tablespoons chicken broth or water
- 1 can (about 8 ounces) baby corn, drained, rinsed, and cut into ½-inch pieces
- 1 green onion (including top), thinly sliced
- 1 cup frozen peas, thawed
- ½ cup sliced fresh mushrooms
- 4 cups cooked brown rice
- 2 tablespoons soy sauce
- 2 tablespoons oyster sauce
- 2 teaspoons sesame oil
- ¼ teaspoon white pepper
- Shredded lettuce for garnish

Place a wok or wide frying pan over high heat until hot. Add the vegetable oil, swirling to coat the sides. Add the garlic, ginger, and onion; cook until the onion is soft, about 30 seconds. Add the carrot, celery, and broth and stir-fry for 2 minutes. Add the baby corn, green onion, peas, mushrooms, and rice, separating the grains of rice with the back of a spoon; mix well. Stir in the soy sauce, oyster sauce, sesame oil, and pepper; cook until heated through. Garnish with shredded lettuce.

TIP: How the rice is cooked in the first place affects the texture of fried rice. If you want the rice to be separate and chewy, use slightly less water; if you prefer it more tender and sticky, use more water.

Golden Rice Rolls

8 dried black mushrooms
1 tablespoon vegetable oil
1 teaspoon minced garlic
1 medium carrot, shredded
1 can (8 ounces) sliced
  bamboo shoots, slivered
¼ pound cooked ham or
  Chinese barbecued pork,
  slivered
3 green onions (including
  tops), slivered
3 cups cooked medium-grain
  rice
2 tablespoons oyster sauce
1 tablespoon soy sauce
1 teaspoon sesame oil
⅛ teaspoon white pepper
2 tablespoons chicken broth,
  if needed
2 tablespoons flour
2 tablespoons water
12 spring roll wrappers,
  6 inches square
Vegetable oil
  for deep-frying
Worcestershire sauce
  for dipping

These golden treats are stuffed with cooked rice, vegetables, and ham. Be sure to use spring roll wrappers; they are thinner than egg roll wrappers and have a crisper, more delicate crust after frying.

Makes 12

1. Soak the mushrooms in warm water to cover for 30 minutes; drain. Cut off and discard the stems and slice the caps into slivers.

2. Place a wok or wide frying pan over high heat until hot. Add the oil, swirling to coat the sides. Add the garlic and cook, stirring, until fragrant, about 10 seconds. Add the carrot and mushrooms and stir-fry for 30 seconds. Add the bamboo shoots, ham, and green onions and cook for 1 minute. Remove from the heat. Add the rice, stirring to separate the grains. Add the oyster sauce, soy sauce, sesame oil, and pepper; mix well. Add the broth if the mixture is too dry. Transfer to a bowl and refrigerate until cool.

3. Combine the flour and water in a small bowl. Lay a wrapper on the table, one corner toward you. Mound about ⅓ cup of the rice mixture across the wrapper (keep the remaining wrappers covered to prevent drying). Fold the bottom corner over the filling to cover it, then fold in the right and left corners. Roll the filled portion over once to enclose the filling. Brush the sides and top of the remaining triangle lightly with flour paste and fold it over to seal the roll. Cover the filled rice rolls with a damp cloth while filling the remaining wrappers.

4. Preheat the oven to 200°. Set a wok in a ring stand and add oil to a depth of about 2 inches. Heat the oil to 360° and adjust the heat to medium-high. Carefully add the rice rolls, a few at a time; cook, turning occasionally, until golden brown, about 3 minutes. Keep the cooked rolls warm in the oven while cooking the remaining rolls. Serve with Worcestershire sauce as a dipping sauce.

Coconut-Curry Shrimp Fried Rice

½ cup shredded coconut
½ cup coarsely chopped
    walnuts

Sauce
¼ cup chicken broth
3 tablespoons soy sauce
1 tablespoon sesame oil
2 teaspoons curry powder
⅛ teaspoon white pepper

❀

2 tablespoons vegetable oil
1 teaspoon minced ginger
½ small onion, cut into
    ¼-inch squares
½ red bell pepper, seeded
    and cut into ¼-inch squares
4 cups cooked
    long-grain rice
½ cup small cooked shrimp
½ cup frozen peas, thawed

Each time I make fried rice, it's a little different. That's the fun of it. The ingredients I use depend upon what I have on hand in my pantry and refrigerator. The wonderful coconut-curry flavor combination in this fried rice comes by way of Southeast Asia.

Serves 4

1. Preheat the oven to 350°. Spread the coconut in a shallow baking pan and toast it in the oven, stirring frequently, until lightly browned, 4 to 5 minutes. Set aside. Spread the walnuts in another shallow baking pan and toast them, stirring frequently, until golden, 8 to 10 minutes. Set aside.

2. Combine the sauce ingredients in a small bowl; set aside.

3. Place a wok or wide frying pan over high heat until hot. Add the oil, swirling to coat the sides. Add the ginger and onion and cook, stirring, until the onion is softened, about 1½ minutes. Add the bell pepper; stir-fry for 1 minute. Reduce the heat to medium and stir in the rice, separating the grains with the back of a spoon. Add the shrimp, peas, and sauce. Cook, stirring, until well blended and heated through. Sprinkle with coconut and walnuts.

TIPS: To keep the individual grains of rice separate in this or any fried rice dish, start with cold, not hot, cooked rice.

Fresh coconut meat can be toasted in the microwave. Grate the flesh of one whole fresh coconut. Place the coconut meat on a microwave-safe dish; cook uncovered on high, stirring occasionally, until toasted, about 10 minutes.

139

Hanoi Beef and Noodle Soup

Marinade

1 tablespoon soy sauce
1 tablespoon dry sherry or
  Chinese rice wine
1 teaspoon sesame oil
1 teaspoon cornstarch

❁

¼ pound boneless tender beef,
  sliced paper-thin
  across the grain
½ pound dried flat rice
  noodles, about ¼ inch wide
1 cup bean sprouts
2 tablespoons slivered
  green onion
Cilantro (Chinese parsley)
  sprigs
3 cups chicken broth
2 thin slices lime
½ fresh serrano or
  jalapeño chile, thinly sliced
1 tablespoon minced
  lemongrass
2 teaspoons fish sauce
1 teaspoon sesame oil
1 teaspoon fresh lime juice

This is fast food, Vietnamese style. Buy paper-thin slices of sukiyaki-style beef so the meat will cook when it comes in contact with the hot broth. If you use thicker slices of beef, stir-fry them briefly or simmer them in the broth for one or two minutes before adding them to the noodles.

Serves 2

1. Combine the marinade ingredients in a medium bowl. Add the beef, stir to coat, and set aside for 30 minutes.

2. Soak the noodles in warm water to cover for 15 minutes or until soft; drain. Divide the noodles between 2 large soup bowls and place half of the beef slices, bean sprouts, green onion, and cilantro in each bowl.

3. In a medium saucepan, bring the broth, lime slices, chile slices, and lemongrass to a boil. Reduce the heat and simmer for 10 minutes. Ladle the hot broth into the bowls of noodles and meat. Season each serving with fish sauce, sesame oil, and lime juice.

TIP: To use lemongrass, cut off the stiff upper leaves, peel away the outer layers at the base, and mince only the bottom 6 inches.

MICROWAVE METHOD: Marinate the beef as directed in step 1. Heat 4 cups of water in a 2-quart microwave-safe bowl on high for 4 minutes. Add the noodles, cover, and cook on high until tender but firm to the bite, about 5 minutes. Drain, rinse, and drain again; place the noodles in a serving bowl with the beef slices, bean sprouts, green onion, and cilantro. Heat the broth, lime, chile, and lemongrass in a 2-quart microwave-safe bowl on high until boiling, about 5 minutes. Pour over the noodles and meat; sprinkle with the fish sauce, sesame oil, and lime juice.

Chicken Chow Fun with Black Bean Sauce

Marinade

2 tablespoons soy sauce
1 tablespoon dry sherry
1 teaspoon cornstarch

✿

½ pound boneless chicken breast

Sauce

¼ cup chicken broth
1 tablespoon soy sauce
1 tablespoon dark soy sauce
1 teaspoon sesame oil
½ teaspoon sugar
½ teaspoon cornstarch
⅛ teaspoon white pepper

✿

2 tablespoons vegetable oil
1 teaspoon minced garlic
1 teaspoon minced ginger
½ teaspoon crushed
   red pepper
2 tablespoons Chinese
   preserved black beans,
   rinsed, drained, and
   coarsely chopped
1 pound fresh rice noodles
¼ pound snow peas,
   ends removed, cut
   in half diagonally
2 green onions, cut into
   1-inch pieces

Chow mein is made with stir-fried wheat-flour noodles. Substitute fresh rice noodles and you have chow fun. These wide, tender noodles cook quickly and need constant stirring to keep them from sticking to the pan. This is one case where a nonstick skillet works even better than a wok. Beef is the traditional meat for chow fun, but it is also delicious with chicken, pork, or seafood.

Serves 6

1. Combine the marinade ingredients in a medium bowl. Skin the chicken and slice it thinly. Add it to the marinade, stir to coat, and set it aside for 30 minutes. Combine the sauce ingredients in a small bowl; set aside.

2. Place a wok or wide frying pan over high heat until hot. Add the oil, swirling to coat the sides. Add the garlic, ginger, red pepper, and black beans and cook until fragrant, about 10 seconds. Add the chicken and stir-fry until opaque, about 2 minutes. Reduce the heat to medium. Add the noodles, snow peas, and green onions. Cook, stirring, for 1 minute. Add the sauce and stir for 1 minute or until well combined.

TIP: Fresh rice noodles (*sha ho fun*) can be found in the refrigerator section of Chinese markets. They come in a large roll of spongy white sheets, which may or may not already be cut into noodles. If not, slice the roll across into strips ½ to ¾ inch wide. They will keep for up to a week in their plastic wrapper in your refrigerator. If you prefer, you can substitute the dried rice noodles described in the recipe for Pad Thai (see page 146), or any other flat noodles.

Steamed "Rice Noodle" Rolls

Marinade
2 egg whites, lightly beaten
2 tablespoons dry sherry or Chinese rice wine
2 teaspoons sesame oil
2 teaspoons soy sauce
2 teaspoons cornstarch

✿

½ pound lean ground beef

Dipping Sauce
¼ cup soy sauce
1 tablespoon hoisin sauce

✿

1½ cups unsifted cake flour
3 tablespoons cornstarch
1 teaspoon salt
2 cups water
¼ cup plus 1 tablespoon vegetable oil
2 green onions (including tops), thinly sliced

In Chinese restaurants these rolls are made from rice flour and cooked in a special rectangular steamer. But you can easily duplicate them at home with cake flour and steam them in your wok.

Makes 10

1. Combine the marinade ingredients in a small bowl. Add the beef, mix well, and set aside for 30 minutes. Combine the dipping sauce ingredients in a small bowl; set aside.

2. To make the noodle batter, sift the flour, cornstarch, and salt together into a medium bowl. Combine the water with ¼ cup of oil and pour it over the flour. Stir until the mixture forms a smooth, thin batter.

3. Place a steaming rack in a wok, pour in water to just below the level of the rack, and bring it to a boil. Rub a 9-inch heatproof glass pie pan with about ¼ teaspoon of oil and pour in ⅓ cup of the batter. Place about 2 tablespoons of the ground beef and a few slices of green onion across the center of the batter. Set the dish on the rack, making sure it is level. Cover and steam for 7 minutes or until the batter is cooked through. Carefully loosen one edge of the noodle with a spatula, then roll it up (if it sticks to the dish, cover and steam for 1 more minute). Transfer the roll to a platter; cook the remaining rolls. Serve at room temperature with the dipping sauce.

VARIATION: You can use Chinese chives rather than green onions and substitute ½ cup of dried shrimp (soaked to soften) or barbecued pork for the beef.

143

Noodle Pancakes with Meat Sauce

Sauce

½ cup chicken broth
2 tablespoons oyster sauce
1 tablespoon soy sauce
1 teaspoon sesame oil
⅛ teaspoon white pepper

Marinade

2 teaspoons soy sauce
2 teaspoons dry sherry or
  Chinese rice wine
1 teaspoon cornstarch

✿

½ pound lean ground turkey
½ pound fresh egg noodles
3 tablespoons vegetable oil
1 teaspoon minced garlic
½ teaspoon crushed red
  pepper
1 Chinese sausage
  (about 2 ounces),
  coarsely chopped
½ cup coarsely chopped
  water chestnuts
2 green onions (including
  tops), finely chopped
2½ teaspoons cornstarch
  dissolved in
  5 teaspoons water

Crispy on the outside, soft and moist on the inside, these noodle pancakes make a wonderful base for any stir-fried dish with gravy. The more oil you use to brown the noodles, the crispier they become.

Serves 4

1. Combine the sauce ingredients in a small bowl; set aside. Combine the marinade ingredients in a medium bowl. Add the turkey, mix well, and set aside for 30 minutes.

2. Cook the noodles according to package directions until tender but firm to the bite. Drain, rinse under cold running water, and drain again.

3. Preheat the oven to 200°. Place a wide frying pan with a nonstick finish over medium-high heat until hot. Add 2 teaspoons of the vegetable oil, swirling to coat the surface. Spread half the noodles over the bottom of the pan. Press the noodles into a firm pancake about 8 inches in diameter. Cook until the bottom is golden brown, about 5 minutes. With a wide spatula, carefully turn the pancake over. Add 1 more teaspoon of vegetable oil around the edges of the pan and cook until the other side is golden brown, about 3 more minutes. Remove the noodle pancake to a large heatproof serving platter and keep it warm in the oven. Repeat with the remaining noodles and 1 more tablespoon of vegetable oil.

4. Place a wok or wide frying pan over high heat until hot. Add the remaining tablespoon of vegetable oil to the wok. Add the garlic, red pepper, and sausage and cook, stirring, for 1 minute. Add the turkey and stir-fry until it is lightly browned and crumbly, about 2 minutes. Add the water chestnuts and green onions and cook 1 minute. Stir in the sauce and add the cornstarch solution. Cook, stirring, until the sauce boils and thickens. Spoon the meat mixture over the noodle pancakes.

TIP: Fresh egg noodles freeze well and do not need to be thawed before cooking.

Pad Thai

½ pound dried flat rice
   noodles, about ¼ inch wide

Sauce
¼ cup chicken broth
3 tablespoons fish sauce
2 tablespoons catsup
2 tablespoons sugar
½ teaspoon crushed
   red pepper

❁

3 tablespoons vegetable oil
1 tablespoon minced garlic
¼ pound lean ground pork
¼ pound medium raw shrimp,
   shelled, deveined, and
   cut in half lengthwise
1 egg, lightly beaten

Garnishes
2 limes, cut into wedges
1 cup bean sprouts
1 green onion (including
   top), thinly sliced
2 tablespoons coarsely
   chopped nuts
2 tablespoons chopped
   cilantro (Chinese parsley)

Thai cooking is hot and trendy. When my good friend Joyce Jue teaches at the Yan Can Cooking School, she always includes this popular Thai favorite in the menu. It's made with fettuccine-like noodles made from rice flour. In typical Thai style, it contrasts hot, sweet, sour, and salty flavors.

Serves 4

1. Soak the noodles in warm water to cover for 15 minutes or until soft; drain and set aside. Combine the sauce ingredients in a small bowl.

2. Place a wok or wide frying pan over high heat until hot. Add the oil, swirling to coat the sides. Add the garlic and cook, stirring, until fragrant, about 10 seconds. Add the pork and stir-fry for 2 minutes. Add the shrimp and stir-fry for 1 minute or until barely pink. Stir in the sauce and cook for 1 minute. Add the noodles; toss to combine them with the sauce, and pour in the egg. Toss continuously until the egg is cooked, about 1 minute.

3. Place the noodle mixture on a serving platter, arrange the lime wedges and bean sprouts around the outside, and sprinkle the green onion, nuts, and cilantro on top.

TIP: You may find these translucent, ¼-inch-wide noodles in bags marked with their Vietnamese name, *banh pho.* If you cannot find them, use Chinese-style fresh egg noodles and cook according to package directions until tender, but firm to the bite.

Savory Noodle Soup

¼ pound fresh egg noodles
1½ cups chicken broth
¼ teaspoon minced ginger
2 tablespoons matchstick pieces Smithfield ham
8 spinach leaves, cut into fine shreds
1 teaspoon soy sauce
⅛ teaspoon sesame oil

Billions of people in China, Japan, and other Asian countries enjoy noodle soup every day. Convenient, simple, and nutritious, noodle soup is one of my favorites, too.

Serves 1

1. Boil the noodles according to package directions until tender but firm to the bite. Drain, rinse under cold running water, and drain again. Place in a deep soup bowl; set aside.

2. In a small saucepan, bring the broth, ginger, and ham to a boil over medium-high heat. Reduce the heat and simmer for 2 minutes. Place the spinach on top of the noodles, sprinkle with soy sauce and sesame oil, and pour the hot broth over all.

TIP: Smithfield ham, a dry-cured ham from Virginia, is the closest equivalent to Chinese Yunnan ham. If it is unavailable, substitute any dry-cured ham, such as prosciutto or Westphalian. As a variation, use matchstick pieces of barbecued pork or cooked chicken.

MICROWAVE METHOD: Heat two cups of water in a 1-quart microwave-safe bowl on high for 2 minutes. Add the noodles, cover, and cook on high until tender but firm to the bite, about 3 minutes. Drain, rinse, and drain again; place the noodles in a serving bowl. In a 1-quart microwave-safe bowl, heat the broth, ginger, and ham on high until boiling, about 2 minutes. Pour over noodles and spinach. Sprinkle with soy sauce and sesame seeds.

Zesty Buckwheat Noodle Salad

Dressing

2 tablespoons chicken broth
5 teaspoons soy sauce
1 tablespoon balsamic
   vinegar or Chinese
   dark rice vinegar
1 tablespoon fresh
   lemon juice
2 teaspoons sesame oil
1½ teaspoons dry sherry or
   Chinese rice wine
¾ teaspoon chili oil
1½ teaspoons sugar

✿

½ pound dried buckwheat
   noodles (soba)
1 small red bell pepper,
   seeded and cut into
   matchstick pieces
1 cup thinly sliced cucumber
2 green onions
   (including tops), cut
   into 1½-inch slivers
2 tablespoons chopped
   cilantro (Chinese parsley)
   or Chinese chives
1 teaspoon white sesame
   seeds, toasted (see page 17)
1 teaspoon black sesame
   seeds (optional)

Buckwheat noodles are popular in Japanese cuisine. I love their chewy texture—it's terrific in salads and soups. This dish resembles the traditional buckwheat noodle dishes served in many Japanese noodle houses; it's great for lunch.

Serves 4

1. Combine the dressing ingredients in a small bowl; set aside.

2. Cook the noodles according to package directions until tender but firm to the bite. Drain, rinse under cold water, and drain again. Place the noodles in a large bowl. Pour half of the dressing over the noodles and toss to coat them evenly. Let them stand about 30 minutes to cool. Just before serving, add the remaining dressing and vegetables and toss to mix evenly. Sprinkle with sesame seeds.

TIPS: If you don't coat the noodles with dressing right after cooking, rinse them in cold water; this helps to keep the noodles from sticking to each other. Don't dress the noodles more than 30 minutes before serving or they will absorb all the dressing.

Just about any vegetable may be used in this recipe; try adding blanched broccoli or cauliflower florets.

Desserts

Desserts

The Chinese have a sweet tooth just like everybody else. However, instead of serving sweets at the end of a meal as people do in the West, we savor them as snacks with tea, or as a special course in a formal banquet. I have included some of my favorites in this chapter.

Almond-Coconut Cheesecake

Crust

1 cup crushed Chinese almond cookies or vanilla wafers

½ cup sweetened flaked or shredded coconut

¼ cup butter or margarine, melted and cooled

Filling

1 pound cream cheese, softened

1 cup sugar

2 tablespoons cornstarch

3 eggs

¾ cup canned unsweetened coconut milk

1 cup sour cream

1½ teaspoons vanilla extract

½ teaspoon almond extract

❀

½ cup toasted sweetened flaked or shredded coconut for garnish

Rich and elegant, this is a cheesecake lover's dream. If I were to give it a Chinese name, I'd call it seven-precious cheesecake. Count the major ingredients and you'll see why. Serve it in small wedges with a cup of fragrant tea.

Serves 10

1. Preheat the oven to 325°. Combine the crust ingredients in a medium bowl until well blended. Press into the bottom of a greased 8-inch springform pan. Bake for 15 minutes and let stand until cool. Leave the oven on.

2. While the crust cools, beat the cream cheese, sugar, and cornstarch in the large bowl of an electric mixer until soft and smooth. Beat in the eggs, one at a time. Add the coconut milk, sour cream, and vanilla and almond extracts and slowly beat just until blended (do not over-beat). Pour the filling into the prepared crust and place the pan on a cookie sheet. Bake until the edges of the cake begin to brown and a knife inserted halfway into the center comes out clean, about one hour. The center will still be slightly jiggly. Turn off the oven, leave the oven door slightly ajar, and allow the cheesecake to cool for 1 hour. Let it cool on a rack to room temperature. Cover and refrigerate for up to 2 days. To serve, remove the pan sides and place the cake on a plate. Sprinkle with coconut before serving.

TIP: Shake the can of coconut milk vigorously before opening.

152

Kiwifruit Almond Shortcake

Dough

2 cups all-purpose flour
2½ teaspoons baking powder
½ teaspoon baking soda
½ teaspoon salt
3 tablespoons sugar
⅓ cup butter or margarine, cut into chunks
3½ ounces almond paste, crumbled
½ cup walnuts
¾ cup plus 3 tablespoons buttermilk

Kiwifruit Sauce

1 ounce rock sugar (about 1-inch square) or 4 teaspoons granulated sugar
1½ cups unsweetened pineapple juice
1 tablespoon tapioca starch dissolved in 2 tablespoons water
8 kiwifruit, peeled and thinly sliced

❀

Black sesame seeds (optional)

Like most Chinese homes, ours did not have an oven; the restaurants in Hong Kong where I learned to cook professionally used their huge ovens to roast poultry and pork. So I had no place for baking. Finally now I have an oven to bake mouthwatering desserts like almond shortcake. I serve the shortcake with an emerald green kiwifruit sauce, then sprinkle black sesame seeds over the top.

Serves 8

1. In a food processor, combine the flour, baking powder, baking soda, salt, and 2 tablespoons of sugar. Process for 10 seconds. Scatter the butter, almond paste, and walnuts over the flour mixture and pulse until the mixture looks crumbly. With the processor running, pour ¾ cup of buttermilk down the feed tube and process until the dough clings together. (Some chunks of almond paste and nuts may remain.)

2. Preheat the oven to 450°. On a lightly floured board, knead the dough for 2 minutes, then pat or roll it out to 1 inch thick. Cut it into eight 3-inch circles. Brush the tops with the remaining buttermilk and sprinkle on the remaining sugar. Place the rounds on a cookie sheet and bake until golden brown, about 20 minutes.

3. To make the sauce, bring the rock sugar and pineapple juice to a boil in a medium saucepan. Reduce the heat and simmer, stirring occasionally, until the sugar is dissolved, about 5 minutes. Add the tapioca solution and cook, stirring, until thickened. Remove from the heat and let stand until cool. Gently stir in the kiwifruit.

4. To serve, split the warm or room temperature shortcakes in half horizontally. Spoon the kiwifruit sauce between the layers and over the top of each shortcake. Sprinkle sesame seeds over the top.

TIP: Rock sugar, a slightly amber-colored sugar in large crystals, is sold in Chinese markets. It gives a mellower sweetness than ordinary granulated sugar.

Fruit in Gingered Plum Wine

¼ cup plum wine
2 tablespoons preserved ginger in syrup, diced, plus 1 tablespoon syrup
1 tablespoon plum sauce
1 small pineapple, cut into ½-inch cubes
1 can (11 ounces) mandarin oranges, drained
3 kiwifruit, peeled and cut into chunks or wedges
Mint sprigs for garnish

Plum and ginger combine to give the fruits in this simple dessert a delicate sweet-hot accent. Kiwifruit (called Sichuan wild gooseberries or monkey fruit in western China) add a lively color. You can add any colorful fruit in season.

Serves 4 to 6

Combine the plum wine, preserved ginger, ginger syrup, and plum sauce in a serving bowl. Add the pineapple and mix well. Add the oranges and kiwifruit and mix gently, just until they are coated with the plum wine mixture. Garnish with mint sprigs.

TIP: Preserved ginger in syrup comes in glass jars or ceramic crocks. Once opened, the tender and sweet ginger will keep indefinitely in a cool place. It is also good chopped and added to baked apples, ice cream, or salads.

Sweet Walnut Soup

1½ cups walnuts
4 cups water
1 tablespoon peanut butter
⅓ cup (packed) brown sugar
½ cup half-and-half or evaporated milk
⅓ cup canned unsweetened coconut milk
¼ cup cornstarch dissolved in ½ cup water

Because of a lack of refrigeration, Chinese cooks developed hot desserts like this sweet soup. It usually contains almonds and sesame seeds; in this version, I've used walnuts and peanut butter.

Serves 8

1. Preheat the oven to 350°. Spread the walnuts in a shallow baking pan. Bake, stirring occasionally, until toasty brown, 10 to 12 minutes. Cool. Combine the nuts, 2 cups of the water, and the peanut butter in a blender. Process until smooth.

2. Combine the brown sugar and the remaining 2 cups of water in a medium saucepan. Cook over high heat until the sugar dissolves. Add the walnut mixture, half-and-half, and coconut milk. Reduce the heat to medium-low. Cook, stirring, just until the mixture simmers. Add the cornstarch solution and cook, stirring, until the soup boils and thickens slightly. Serve hot or warm.

Lemon Rice Pudding

3 cups cooked long-grain
   rice
3 cups milk, whole or
   low-fat
¾ cup sugar
2 tablespoons finely chopped
   crystallized ginger
1 teaspoon grated
   lemon peel
¼ cup coarsely chopped
   walnuts
1 teaspoon vanilla extract

As much as we love rice in China, you won't find rice pudding there. Since I moved to the West, I have learned to love it. This light, lemony version is a healthful and delicious way to end your meal.

Serves 4 to 6

Combine the rice, milk, and sugar in a 2-quart saucepan; bring to a boil over medium-high heat. Reduce the heat to medium-low and simmer, stirring to break up any rice lumps, for 20 minutes. Add the ginger and lemon peel and simmer, stirring frequently, until the mixture thickens, about 10 minutes. Remove from the heat and stir in the walnuts and vanilla. Serve warm.

TIPS: To reheat the pudding, stir in several tablespoons of milk and warm in a saucepan over low heat. Or reheat in a microwave oven.

For an attractive presentation, lightly pack the pudding into a lightly greased 4-cup mold. Let it stand for 5 minutes before inverting it onto a serving plate to unmold.

Gladys's Sweet Wontons

Filling
¼ cup shredded coconut
¼ cup raisins or pitted
   prunes, chopped
¼ cup chopped walnuts
¼ cup sugar
2 tablespoons black
   sesame seeds
2 tablespoons white
   sesame seeds
½ teaspoon cinnamon

You can thank my friend Gladys for these sweet treats. A culinary expert—and a born innovator—she has a way with wontons. These make a wonderful dim sum snack or a sweet contribution to a buffet.

Makes about 2 dozen

1. Combine the filling ingredients in a medium bowl; set aside. Place 1 teaspoon of filling in the center of a wonton wrapper (keep the remaining wrappers covered to prevent drying). Brush the edges of the wrapper lightly with egg. Fold it in half over the filling to form a triangle; press the edges firmly to seal. Repeat with the remaining filling and wrappers. As you work, place the filled wontons slightly apart on a baking sheet and

❀

About 2 dozen wonton
   wrappers
1 egg, beaten
Vegetable oil for
   deep-frying

cover them with a damp cloth until all are filled.

2. Set a wok in a ring stand and add oil to a depth of about 2 inches. Heat the oil to 360° and adjust the heat to medium-high. Fry the wontons, a few at a time, turning them occasionally, until golden brown, about 2 minutes. Lift them out and drain them on paper towels.

VARIATION: For a chocolate treat, use ¼ cup semisweet chocolate chips and ½ teaspoon grated orange peel in place of the raisins.

Flambéed Tropical Fruit

1 fresh mango OR 1 can
   (15 ounces) mango slices
   in light syrup
¼ cup butter or margarine
¼ cup (packed) brown sugar
1 teaspoon minced ginger
¼ teaspoon ground allspice
2 firm, ripe bananas, peeled,
   halved lengthwise, and cut
   diagonally into 1-inch
   pieces
¼ cup cognac
1 pint vanilla ice cream
1 tablespoon chopped
   crystallized ginger

This is the kind of dish that's fun to do on television. It always gets "oohs" and "aahs." You'll win rave reviews at home, too. Assemble the sauce ingredients on a tray, pull out your chafing dish or electric skillet, dim the lights, and flame this at the table for your guests.

Serves 4

1. Peel the mango and cut the meat from the pit (or drain canned mango); cut the meat into ½-inch-wide strips. In a wide frying pan, melt the butter over medium heat with the brown sugar, ginger, and allspice. When the butter is melted and the mixture begins to bubble, add the bananas and mango slices and stir gently to coat the fruit with sauce. Cook for 1 minute.

2. Measure the cognac into a small heatproof bowl and microwave it for 5 seconds or place it in a small pan and heat it over high heat until bubbly. Add to the frying pan, light with a long-handled match, and spoon the liqueur over the fruit until the flames die. Scoop the ice cream into serving dishes and top each serving with some fruit mixture and a sprinkling of crystallized ginger.

Tangerine Champagne Sorbet

1 envelope (1 tablespoon)
  unflavored gelatin
¼ cup cold water
1 can (12 ounces) frozen
  tangerine juice concentrate,
  thawed
¼ cup sugar
2 cups champagne
2 tablespoons orange-
  flavored liqueur
1 tablespoon fresh
  lemon juice
3 tablespoons grated
  tangerine or orange peel
2 egg whites

This sorbet looks very pretty served in Chinese tea cups. The concentrated fruitiness makes an especially satisfying ending to a Chinese meal of diverse flavors.

Serves 8

1. Sprinkle the gelatin over the cold water in a small bowl. Let it soften for 5 minutes.

2. Bring the tangerine juice concentrate and sugar to a boil in a saucepan over medium heat. Stir until the sugar is dissolved. Reduce the heat to low. Add the softened gelatin and stir until dissolved. Remove from the heat.

3. After letting the mixture cool slightly, stir in the champagne, liqueur, lemon juice, and tangerine peel. Cover and refrigerate until cold but not thick, about 30 minutes.

4. Beat the egg whites until frothy and fold them into the chilled tangerine mixture. Transfer to an ice cream freezer and freeze according to the manufacturer's directions. Serve immediately or store in the freezer for up to one week.

Walnut Lace Cookies

½ cup butter or margarine
⅔ cup (packed) brown sugar
½ cup light corn syrup
1 cup all-purpose flour
½ cup finely chopped
  walnuts

The intricate patterns in these cookies remind me of the beautiful baskets made in China. When warm, the cookies are flexible enough to be curled, rolled, or folded. The cooled cookies are crisp and brittle.

Makes about 3 dozen

1. Preheat the oven to 375°. Combine the butter, brown sugar, and corn syrup in a small saucepan. Cook, stirring, over medium heat until the sugar dissolves and the mixture begins to bubble. Remove from the heat and stir well. Gradually beat in the flour. Add the nuts. Keep the batter warm by setting the saucepan in a larger pan filled with 2 inches of barely simmering water.

2. Drop the batter by teaspoonfuls, about 3 inches apart, onto a lightly greased baking sheet. Allow 3 or 4 cookies per sheet. Bake until the edges of the cookies are golden brown, 4 to 5 minutes. If you're going to leave the cookies flat, let them cool until firm, about 5 minutes. If you want to shape them, bake only one sheet at a time and let the cookies cool until they are firm enough to remove from the pan but are still soft enough to role or curl, less than a minute. Transfer the finished cookies to racks to cool, then store in an airtight container.

Kiwifruit Fritters

¾ cup all-purpose flour
1 tablespoon sugar
1½ teaspoons baking powder
1 teaspoon Chinese
   five-spice
⅔ cup water
1 tablespoon vegetable oil
1 teaspoon black sesame
   seeds
6 kiwifruit, each peeled and
   cut into 6 wedges
1 tablespoon cornstarch
Vegetable oil for
   deep-frying
Powdered sugar

During my student days at the University of California at Davis, I taught Chinese cooking to stretch my meager budget. I'd buy kiwifruit by the dozen and experiment, making desserts to satisfy the sweet tooth of my students. Kiwifruit fritters were an instant hit. They are similar to the deep-fried apples I ate growing up in China.

Serves 6 to 8

1. Stir together the flour, sugar, baking powder, and five-spice in a medium bowl. Gradually stir in the water. Add the vegetable oil and blend with a wire whisk until smooth. Cover and refrigerate for 2 hours. Stir in the sesame seeds. Pat the kiwifruit wedges dry with paper towels. Sprinkle them with cornstarch just before you are ready to cook them.

2. Set a wok in a ring stand and add oil to a depth of about 2 inches. Heat the oil to 375° and adjust the heat to medium-high. Using chopsticks or a fork to spear them, dip the kiwifruit slices into the batter. Let the excess batter drip off, then gently lower the fruit into the hot oil. Stirring occasionally, cook several pieces at a time until golden brown and puffy, about 2 minutes. Lift the fritters out and drain them on paper towels. Sprinkle with powdered sugar. Serve warm.

Steamed Kiwifruit Upside-Down Cake

8 kiwifruit, peeled and
    sliced ¼ inch thick
1¾ cups (packed)
    light brown sugar
2 cups cake flour
1 tablespoon baking powder
1 teaspoon baking soda
5 eggs
¾ cup evaporated milk
½ cup (¼ pound) butter,
    melted and cooled
¼ teaspoon almond extract

Most Chinese homemakers steam their cakes; I learned how from my Mom. I like to make this delicious kiwi-topped cake for her on Mother's Day.

Makes one 9-inch cake

1. Lightly coat a 9- by 2-inch round cake pan with vegetable cooking spray. Line the bottom of the pan with parchment or wax paper. Coat again with vegetable cooking spray. Set aside.

2. Arrange the kiwifruit slices in the cake pan and sprinkle them with ¾ cup of brown sugar. Sift the flour, baking powder, and baking soda together into a medium bowl; set aside. Beat the eggs and the remaining 1 cup brown sugar in the bowl of an electric mixer at medium speed for 5 minutes or until thick and creamy. Add the evaporated milk, butter, and almond extract; beat on low speed for 1 minute. Using a rubber spatula, gradually fold in the flour mixture until well blended. Spoon a small amount of the batter carefully over the kiwifruit, then gently pour in the remaining batter.

3. Place a bamboo steamer in a wok, add water to just below the level of the steamer, and bring to a boil. Carefully set the cake pan in the steamer, making sure it is level. Cover and steam, adding additional water to the wok if necessary, until a wooden pick inserted in the center of the cake comes out clean, about 30 minutes. Remove the cake from the steamer and let it cool in the pan for 20 minutes. Turn it upside down onto a serving platter; remove the pan and parchment. Serve slightly warm.

Glossary of Ingredients

Chinese and other Asian cooking has become so popular in the West that most supermarkets carry a wide variety of Asian foods. You should have no trouble finding most of the ingredients used in this book. For a wider selection and for some of the more unusual ingredients, you may wish to visit your nearest Asian grocery.

Bamboo Shoots

Whole or sliced bamboo shoots, used for their slightly sweet flavor and crunchy texture, are available in cans and occasionally fresh wherever there are large Asian communities. Store any leftovers in a glass jar in the refrigerator, covered with water. Change the water every couple of days.

Barbecued Pork, Chinese

Called *char siu* in the Cantonese dialect, these shiny red, sweet, highly seasoned strips of roast pork are sold in Chinese delicatessens.

Bean Curd

See Tofu (page 168)

Bean Sprouts

Fresh mung bean sprouts are available in most supermarkets. Choose sprouts that are plump and crisp, without any browning on the tails. They are best used the day you buy them, but they will keep for a day or two in the refrigerator.

Black Beans, Preserved

These small black beans, salted and fermented until soft, are a staple of Cantonese cooking. Rinse, then crush them lightly to release their pungent flavor before adding them to sauces or stir-fried dishes. After opening, store in an airtight container.

Bok Choy

"Bok" means white in Chinese. This member of the cabbage family has long, mild-tasting white stalks. The leaves are dark green and similar to chard in flavor. Dried bok choy is available in Chinese groceries and is widely used in soups.

Cabbage, Chinese (Napa)

Also known as Chinese celery cabbage, it grows in a compact, elongated, yellowish-green head with crinkled fringes. It is slightly sweeter than head cabbage.

162

Chiles	See Peppers, Chile (page 165)
Chili Oil	This hot, reddish-orange oil is infused with dried red chile peppers. It is used as a condiment and as a flavoring ingredient.
Chili Paste, Chinese	Chinese markets sell an amazing array of bottled and canned pastes and sauces based on dried chiles. Some also contain brown or black beans, while those labeled Sichuan or Szechwan chili paste typically contain a lot of garlic. Brands vary in intensity and flavor, so adjust recipe amounts accordingly.
Chinese Chives	See Tip, page 113.
Daikon	See Tip, page 99.
Fish Sauce	This thin, brown, salty sauce is used as an all-purpose flavoring in southeast Asia and in southern China. Its aroma is stronger than its taste, which mellows with cooking. It is called *nam pla* in Thailand and *nuoc mam* in Vietnam; the Thai variety is most commonly available here.
Five-Spice, Chinese	This all-purpose seasoning is made from a blend of five (or more) ground spices, usually star anise or anise seeds, cloves, cinnamon, fennel, and Sichuan peppercorns.
Ginger	Unless otherwise specified, ginger in one of my recipes always means the fresh ginger "root" (actually a rhizome, a thickened underground runner). Choose the hardest specimens you can find, without any wrinkles on the skin or evidence of mold. Ginger keeps well in the refrigerator if wrapped in a paper towel and sealed in a plastic bag. You can also freeze it and slice off pieces as you need them; however, the texture will not be as firm after freezing and thawing.
Herbs, Fresh	Cilantro, otherwise known as fresh coriander or Chinese parsley, is the most common fresh herb in Chinese cooking. Some of my Southeast Asian recipes also call for mint or basil. To store these and other fresh herbs,

163

rinse them and place the stems or root ends in a small glass or jar; cover the green tops with a plastic bag and store in the refrigerator.

Hoisin Sauce

This thick, sweet, dark brown sauce is made from soybeans, usually flavored with vinegar, sugar, garlic, and spices. It is used mainly as a barbecue sauce, but is also used as a condiment or seasoning sauce in beef and lamb dishes. Refrigerate in a glass jar after opening.

Lemongrass

One of the most popular herbs in Southeast Asian cooking, lemongrass is valued for its subtle yet compelling lemony flavor. The stiff, fibrous, yellow-green stalks grow up to two feet tall, but only the bottom 6 to 8 inches are tender enough to eat—after being finely sliced, chopped, or pounded to a paste in a mortar. (The tops make a delicious herbal tea.) Wrapped well in plastic, lemongrass stalks will keep for a long time in the refrigerator.

Mushrooms and Other Fungi

Asian cooks use many varieties of dried and fresh mushrooms and fungi. Many are available in supermarkets. Unless otherwise noted, in this book "fresh mushrooms" refers to the familiar cultivated kind; other mushrooms are identified by name.

Dried black mushrooms: Known as *shiitake* in Japanese, these are rich, meaty-flavored mushrooms with wide, flat caps. Soak them in warm water for 30 minutes to soften, then gently squeeze out the excess moisture and cut off and discard the stems. Fresh shiitake mushrooms are more delicate, but Chinese cooks prefer the flavorful dried ones.

Oyster mushrooms: These relatives of shiitake mushrooms are available fresh in some supermarkets and in Japanese markets. They are also available canned in Chinese stores. They are often grilled, stir-fried, and used in soups and salads.

Straw mushrooms: These are light brown, with caps resembling partially opened umbrellas; they are grown

164

on a bed of rice straw. They are available peeled and unpeeled in cans from China; Chinese chefs prefer the unpeeled ones for their texture and richer flavor.

Noodles, Bean Thread See Tip, page 104.

Noodles, Egg In Chinese, *mein* covers a wide range of wheat-flour noodles, fresh and dried, with and without egg. I have simply specified "fresh egg noodles" in this book, so use whatever wheat-flour noodles are available to you. Fresh Chinese-style egg noodles are now sold in many supermarkets, and Asian markets sell many varieties both fresh and dried. The eggless Japanese *udon* are another option.

Noodles, Rice Dried noodles made from rice flour, also called rice sticks or rice vermicelli, are sold in Asian groceries in a variety of widths. Like bean threads, they need just a quick soaking in boiling water to soften them for use in soups or stir-fried dishes. They can also be deep-fried right from the package.

Oil (See also sesame oil, chili oil.) Except where a particular oil is specified for flavoring purposes, the recipes in this book simply call for "vegetable oil." For most cooking, including stir-frying and deep-frying, peanut oil is the favorite oil in China; other unsaturated vegetable oils, including walnut, corn, soybean, safflower, and sunflower, may also be used.

Oyster Sauce This thick, brown, all-purpose seasoning sauce, widely used in Cantonese dishes, is often labeled "oyster flavored sauce." It is made from an extract of oysters, sugar, salt, and starch, usually darkened with caramel color. Refrigerate after opening.

Peppercorns, Sichuan These dried red-brown berries are unrelated to black pepper. Spicy and fragrant, they are pleasantly numbing rather than peppery hot. To bring out their distinctive aroma, toast them in a frying pan over medium heat until quite fragrant, shaking the pan frequently. Use whole or grind in a mortar or spice grinder.

Peppers, Chile

Hot chile peppers are used in many regions of China and in most Southeast Asian cuisines. Although chiles are of New World origin, many Asian countries have bred their own typical varieties. Use whatever variety you like. In general, the smaller the chile, the hotter the flavor; serrano chiles are hotter than the slightly larger jalapeños, and the tiny Thai or Vietnamese "bird" chiles are even hotter. In the recipes, "whole dried chiles" refers to small (1½- to 2-inch long) dried red chiles, either serrano or a similar Asian variety. Add them whole to the wok to flavor the oil for a stir-fried dish or, for a hotter flavor, break them up or use crushed red pepper.

Be careful not to touch your eyes after handling chiles; the volatile oils (especially abundant in the ribs or "veins") can cause a painful burn. If your skin is especially sensitive, you might want to wear rubber or plastic gloves when handling chiles.

Rice

Rice comes in many varieties and shapes, including long, medium, and short grains. Choosing which to use is largely a matter of taste, habit, and the particular recipe. Longer-grained rice cooks drier and with separate grains. Shorter types cook to a softer and stickier consistency. Chinese cooks never use parboiled (converted) or "instant" rice, or add oil or salt when cooking the rice. To save leftover rice, fluff it to separate the kernels, then store it in the refrigerator in an airtight container. Leftover rice is ideal for fried rice, or you can simply reheat it in a steamer or a microwave oven.

Glutinous (sweet) rice: A short-grain rice variety that becomes sticky and slightly transparent when cooked. It requires less water to cook. It is usually combined with other ingredients to make dumplings, stuffings, or desserts.

Sausage, Chinese	Chinese sausages, called *lop cheong* in Cantonese, are made mostly with pork and pork fat (sometimes duck liver is added). Seasoned with sugar, wine, and salt, they have a sweet, full-bodied but never spicy taste. They are sold in 6-inch links tied together in pairs and can be stored in the refrigerator or freezer for long periods. A recipe for a homemade version appears on page 86.
Sesame Oil	Chinese-style sesame oil is a dark, fragrant oil pressed from toasted sesame seeds; it is used in small quantities as a flavoring agent. Look for bottles labeled 100 percent pure sesame oil; many brands are blended with soybean oil, which dilutes the special flavor of sesame oil. The pure variety is more expensive, but worth the price. Keep it in the refrigerator for long storage. Don't confuse Chinese-style sesame oil with the light-colored, cold-pressed sesame oil sold in health food stores; the latter is fine for cooking, but it does not have the same aroma or flavor as the Chinese type.
Sesame Seeds	Sesame seeds are commonly used to flavor Chinese dishes. Often they are toasted and sprinkled over the top of a dish shortly before it is served. The Chinese use black as well as white sesame seeds. Black sesame seeds do not need to be toasted. To toast white sesame seeds, place them in a small skillet over medium heat. Cook, shaking the pan, for 2 to 3 minutes or until the seeds are fragrant and toasty brown.
Shrimp, Dried	These are small shrimp preserved in brine and then dried. Their strong fish flavor enhances vegetable dishes and soups. Soak them in warm water for 30 minutes to soften before using. Store dried shrimp in the refrigerator in an airtight container.
Soy Sauce	Good soy sauce is an essential ingredient in Chinese and Japanese cooking. Unless otherwise specified in a recipe, use a naturally fermented soy sauce (the most widely available is Kikkoman). You may use a reduced-sodium version if you prefer. Chemically hydrolized

soy sauces are not recommended. Occasionally dark soy sauce is specified. Dark soy sauce is exclusively Chinese. It is thicker and darker because it contains molasses. Use it in stews and dishes where richer colors and flavors are desired.

Tangerine Peel, Dried

Available in small cellophane packages, dried tangerine peel has a pungent, sweet, citrus aroma. Soak it to soften before using. Fresh orange peel may be substituted.

Taro

A common starchy staple in southern China and other parts of Southeast Asia, this root vegetable has ringed, hairy brown skin and cream-colored flesh specked with purple. It is usually steamed until just tender, then fried or used in stews, casseroles, or puddings. Taro is used in many of the same ways you would use potatoes.

Tofu

Tofu is the Japanese name for bean curd, a highly nutritious, semisolid cake made from the "milk" extracted from soybeans. Fresh, it is creamy-white, with a smooth, custard-like texture and mild flavor. Commonly sold in plastic tubs, it also comes in vacuum-packed pouches or foil-lined cartons that can be stored at room temperature. Refrigerate fresh tofu and vacuum-packed tofu after opening, covered with cold water. If the water is changed daily, tofu will keep for three to four days. Tofu is often labeled firm, medium, or soft; the soft is especially nice in soups.

Vinegar, Rice

Unless otherwise specified, "rice vinegar" refers to the clear or "white" milder variety, with acidity around 4 to 4.3 percent rather than the regular distilled white vinegar with an acidity of 5 percent. Japanese rice vinegar is widely available and very good. Seasoned rice vinegar is used mainly in preparing sushi and contains sugar. Chinese dark rice vinegar is dark brown, richly colored, and full bodied, with a caramel flavor; Chinkiang vinegar from eastern China is an example. Balsamic vinegar may be substituted for dark rice vinegar.

Wine, Chinese Rice

Shao Hsing, normally 36 to 40 proof, is one of China's most famous drinking wines, and is used in many stir-fried dishes. Made from fermented rice, it is slightly sweet, with a nutty flavor. Dry sherry and Japanese *sake* are close substitutes. The rice wine used in Cantonese cooking is normally 60 to 80 proof.

Wrappers

Chinese and Southeast Asians love to enclose bits of food in wrappers. Many sizes, shapes, and types are available in supermarket produce sections and in Asian grocery stores. When working with wrappers, cover them with a damp cloth to prevent drying.

Six-inch-square *egg roll wrappers* are available in most supermarkets, and are commonly used for Chinese-American-style egg rolls. Most Chinese chefs prefer the thinner *spring roll wrappers,* 8 inches square or sometimes round, which give a crisper texture than egg roll wrappers. They can be purchased in most Asian grocery stores. They are called lumpia wrappers in Filipino cuisine. Wonton wrappers, usually 3½ inches square and varying in thickness, are available in supermarkets. The thinner ones preferred by the Chinese are available only in Chinese stores.

Phyllo-thin *rice paper wrappers* are used for *cha gio,* Vietnamese spring rolls. They are available in many sizes, but 7- to 8-inch rounds are best for *cha gio.* The thin, brittle wrappers need to be carefully softened in liquid before rolling.

Index of Shows

170

Index

Italic page numbers indicate photographs.

Metric Conversion Table

Follow this chart to convert the measurements in this book to their approximate metric equivalents. The metric amounts have been rounded; the slight variations in the conversion rate will not significantly change the recipes.

Liquid and Dry Volume	Metric Equivalent	Temperature	
		°Fahrenheit	°Celsius
1 teaspoon	5 ml	155	70
1 tablespoon (3 teaspoons)	15 ml	165	75
¼ cup	60 ml	185	85
⅓ cup	80 ml	200	95
½ cup	125 ml	275	135
1 cup	250 ml	300	150
		325	160
Weight		350	175
1 ounce	28 grams	375	190
¼ pound	113 grams	400	205
½ pound	225 grams	450	230
1 pound	450 grams		

Linear

1 inch   2.5 cm

Other Helpful Conversion Factors

Sugar, Rice, Flour	1 teaspoon = 10 grams
	1 cup = 220 grams
Cornstarch, Salt	1 teaspoon = 5 grams
	1 tablespoon = 15 grams

Yan Can Cook
Sponsors:

DIAMOND
WALNUTS

萬 KIKKOMAN

TAYLOR & NG
INTERNATIONAL
COOKWARE

Special thanks to:
Iwatani Gourmet Stoves
Petrini's Markets

Yan Can & Company
offers a selection of
additional gourmet
merchandise and cooking
classes through the
Yan Can International
Cooking School.
For details write or phone:
**Yan Can & Company
P.O. Box 4755
Foster City, CA 94404**
415/574-7788